"God will have a free people,
and while we have a duty to perform
to preach the Gospel, we have another to perform,
that is, to stand up in the defence
of human rights—in the defence of our own rights,
the rights of our children, and in defence
of the rights of this nation and of all men,
no matter who they may be,
and God being our helper to maintain
those principles and to lift up a standard
for the honorable of this and other nations to flock to,
that they may be free from the tyranny
and oppression that is sought
to be crowded upon them. This is a duty we have to
perform, and in the name of Israel's God we will do it."
(President John Taylor,
Journal of Discourses 23:239.)

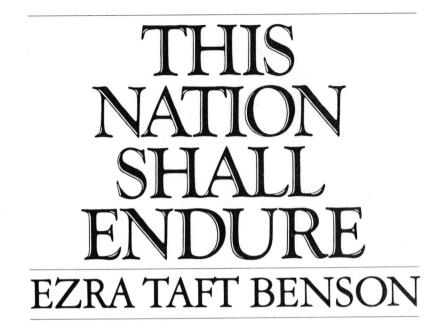

THIS NATION SHALL ENDURE

EZRA TAFT BENSON

Deseret Book Company
Salt Lake City, Utah
1977

Library of Congress Cataloging in Publication Data
Benson, Ezra Taft.
    This nation shall endure.

    Includes index.
    1. Mormons and Mormonism—Addresses, essays, lectures.
2. United States—Civilization—Addresses, essays,
lectures.   I. Title.
BX8639.B42T47   289.3   77-21466
ISBN 0-87747-658-6

Contents

Our Glorious Heritage

*"If we truly cherish
the heritage we have received,
we must maintain the same virtues and . . .
character of our stalwart forebears—
faith in God,
courage, industry, frugality,
self-reliance, and integrity.
We have the obligation to maintain
what those who pledged their lives, their fortunes,
and their sacred honor
gave to future generations."*

America's Debt to Great Britain

"Freedom-loving men owe a debt of gratitude to Great Britain and those human instruments who provided that first flicker of 'freedom's holy light' to future generations, and which made the restoration of the fullness of the gospel possible."

In spite of the serious problems facing Great Britain, one cannot step upon that land and tread its walkways without a supreme consciousness of history. The British Isles are saturated with history. The Western world and free men everywhere owe to England a great debt of gratitude for a legacy handed down over the centuries.

Following the great apostasy from the principles and laws of Christ, the world became enslaved in a cloak of darkness. This long night of Christian apostasy placed an oppressive tyranny on the minds of men, which were shackled by chains of false priestly tradition. Before the gospel could shine forth its resplendent light, a flickering flame of religious and political freedom had to commence somewhere. Heaven determined that it begin in England.

The stage had been set premortally. The characters in the drama had been held in reserve to come at appropriate times and intervals to influence the course of events in history.

A great soul was sent to the earth at Wickliff, New Richmond, in Yorkshire about 1324. His name—John Wycliffe. His voice in later years was raised against the abuses of the church of his day. He was subsequently excommunicated, the most serious offense being that he translated the Bible into the English language. He believed that "the scriptures are the property of the people, and one which no one should be allowed to wrest from them." As a result of his courageous efforts, England for the first time in history was given a complete version of the scriptures in her native language, though published in manuscript form only. In the perspective of time, the efforts of Wycliffe brought about the Great Reformation, and he was given the appropriate title "The Morning Star of the Reformation."

A century later another figure was born in England—William Tyndale. Where Wycliffe's Bible was only a translation of the Latin into English, Tyndale translated his version from the original Greek. The result was the first printed New Testament in English. Utilizing one of the greatest inventions of man, the printing press, the Tyndale New Testament was printed in Germany, smuggled into England, and made available to the English people. For this, Tyndale was strangled and his body burned at the stake. His last words were "Lord, open the King of England's eyes," a prayer that was subsequently answered when King James, son of Mary, Queen of Scots, gave to the world the authorized King James Version of the Bible—the version used to this day by The Church of Jesus Christ of Latter-day Saints.

It was this flicker of freedom and the belief that each man had a right to the possession of God's word that sponsored the Great Reformation in Europe. Speaking of this great movement, and the reformers themselves, President Joseph Fielding Smith wrote: "In preparation for [the restoration of the gospel] the Lord raised up noble men . . . whom we call reformers, and gave them power to break the shackles which bound the people and denied them the sacred right to worship God according to the dictates of conscience. . . .

"In the days of greatest spiritual darkness, when evil raged, the Lord raised up honorable men, who rebelled against the tyranny of the [adversary] and his emissaries. . . ." (*Doctrines of Salvation*, Bookcraft, 1954, 1:174-75. Italics in original.)

President Smith also wrote: "Praise be to the great souls who conducted the Protestant Revolution. They helped to make it possible for the establishment of The Church of Jesus Christ of Latter-day Saints in the early part of the nineteenth century, preparatory to the second coming of the Son of God. For all the good they did we honor them, and they shall receive their reward which shall be great. They were not restorers, but were sent to prepare the way for one who was yet to come with a mission of restoration and everlasting power." (*Essentials in Church History*, Deseret Book, 1950, p. 18.)

Religious freedom cannot prosper where political freedom does not exist. Again, history records that the spark which kindled the flame of political liberty among men commenced in Great Britain. Somewhat over a century before Wycliffe's birth, an event took place in England that opened the door to a recognition of man's rights by abridging the power of the king. Until then, human rights were looked upon as something a monarch might grant to his subjects. On the soil of Runnymede in the year 1215, the English monarch, King John, formally recognized in writing that he had encroached on man's sacred rights, and thus one of history's most influential documents was born, the Great Charter. Since that time this document, also known as the Magna Carta, has become a symbol for man's freedom.

For man to exercise fully the agency God has granted to him, his God-given natural rights must be recognized and protected. It has only been recognized within the past four hundred years that these rights inherently belong to man. It was historical documents such as the English Petition of Rights and the English Bill of Rights that first recognized the "immemorial rights of Englishmen." I believe these movements were inspired of the Lord. Later these God-given rights were to become guaranteed by New World documents, such as the Declaration of Independence and the American Bill of Rights.

Speaking of the circumstances that brought about the principle of self-government, President Brigham Young said on one occasion: "The King of Great Britain . . . might . . . have been led to . . . aggressive acts, for aught we know, to bring to pass the purposes of God, in thus establishing a new government upon a principle of greater freedom, a basis of self-government allowing the free exercise of religious worship." (*Journal of Discourses* 2:170.)

Once a man's rights became guaranteed by the political institutions that would serve him, the time became propitious for the Prophet Joseph Smith to be sent on the world scene, and for the kingdom of God to be restored by direct divine intervention in the year 1830. A light had burst forth among men again, and it was the fullness of the gospel! (See D&C 45:28.)

Yes, freedom-loving men owe a debt of gratitude to Great Britain and those human instruments who provided that first flicker of "freedom's holy light" to future generations, and which made the restoration of the fullness of the gospel possible.

The greatest legacy contributed by the British Isles to the kingdom of God is not appreciated or recognized outside The Church of Jesus Christ of Latter-day Saints. This legacy is the number of valiant souls—veritable defenders of the faith—who have come from the United Kingdom to strengthen the Church at a time of its greatest vulnerability. Until 1837, the Church was largely confined to the United States, principally in the states of Ohio and Missouri. Then a crisis came on the infant church. Many began to apostatize, including some of the leading figures. Speaking of this period, the Prophet Joseph Smith wrote:

"At this time the spirit of speculation in lands and property of all kinds, which was so prevalent throughout the whole nation, was taking deep root in the Church. As the fruits of this spirit, evil surmisings, fault-finding, disunion, dissension, and apostasy followed in quick succession, and it seemed as though all the powers of earth and hell were combining their influence in an especial manner to overthrow the Church at once, and make a final end. . . .

"In this state of things, and but a few weeks before the Twelve were expecting to meet in full quorum, . . . God revealed to me that something new must be done for the salvation of His Church." (*History of the Church* 2:487-89.)

That "something new" which would be "done for the salvation of His Church" was the bringing of the gospel to the British Isles. President Spencer W. Kimball's grandfather, Heber C. Kimball, related the circumstances of this revelation in these words: "On Sunday, the 4th day of June, 1837, the Prophet Joseph came to me, while I was seated in front of the stand, above the sacrament table, on the Melchizedek side of the Temple, in Kirtland, and whispering to me, said, 'Brother Heber, the Spirit of the Lord whispered to me: "Let my servant Heber go to England and proclaim my Gospel, and open the door of salvation to that nation." ' " (Orson F. Whitney, *Life of Heber C. Kimball,* Stevens and Wallis, 1945, pp. 103-4.)

So in 1837, four servants of God were called to the British Isles: Elder Heber C. Kimball, Elder Orson Hyde, Elder Willard Richards, and a priest, Joseph Fielding. Others were to follow, including Brigham Young and Wilford Woodruff. In 1841 Brigham Young wrote:

"We landed in the spring of 1840, as strangers in a strange land and penniless, but through the mercy of God we have gained many friends, established Churches in almost every noted town and city in the kingdom of Great Britain, baptized between seven and eight thousand, printed 5,000 Books of Mormon, 3,000 Hymn Books, 2,500 [copies] of the *Millennial Star,* and 50,000 tracts, and emigrated to Zion 1,000 souls, established a permanent shipping agency, which will be a great blessing to the Saints, and have left sown in the hearts of many thousands the seeds of eternal truth, which will bring forth fruit to the honor and glory of God, and yet we have lacked nothing to eat, drink, or wear: in all these things I acknowledge the hand of God." (*Millennial Star* 26:7.)

One of the most memorable of these experiences, which illustrates how the Lord had prepared a people to receive His gospel, was recorded by Elder Woodruff. He had been directed by the Spirit to the John Benbow farm in Herefordshire, England, in early 1840. Here are his words:

"When I arose to speak at Brother Benbow's house, a man

entered the door and informed me that he was a constable, and had been sent by the rector of the parish with a warrant to arrest me. I asked him, 'For what crime?' He said, 'For preaching to the people.' I told him that I, as well as the rector, had a license for preaching the gospel to the people, and that if he would take a chair I would wait upon him after meeting. He took my chair and sat beside me. For an hour and a quarter I preached the first principles of the everlasting gospel. The power of God rested upon me, the spirit filled the house, and the people were convinced. At the close of the meeting I opened the door for baptism, and seven offered themselves. Among the number were four preachers and the constable. The latter arose and said, 'Mr. Woodruff, I would like to be baptized.' I told him I would like to baptize him. . . .

"The first thirty days after my arrival in Herefordshire, I had baptized forty-five preachers and one hundred and sixty members of the United Brethren, who put into my hands one chapel and forty-five houses, which were licensed according to law to preach in. This opened a wide field of labor, and enabled me to bring into the Church, through the blessings of God, over eighteen hundred souls during eight months, including all of the six hundred United Brethren except one person." (Matthias F. Cowley, *Life of Wilford Woodruff,* Deseret News, 1909, pp. 118-19.)

During this period between 1840 and 1846, it is estimated that over 3,300 Saints from Great Britain, at great personal sacrifice, immigrated to Nauvoo in an effort to give their all to the building of the kingdom of God. Among those early stalwart converts from England were such illustrious names as John Taylor, third president of the Church; George Q. Cannon, counselor in the First Presidency; John R. Winder, counselor in the First Presidency; and George Teasdale, apostle.

Since that time, it has been estimated by the Church Genealogical Society that eighty percent of the members of the Church today are descendants or converts from the British Isles. How the Lord has favored that land and that people by the number of the blood of Israel He has placed there!

My purpose in recounting some of this background is to recall the long historic struggle for the recognition of man's God-given right to worship God according to the dictates of his conscience. God has guided significant events in times past to preserve those rights. He has raised up the individuals with the courage and intrepid will to do what needed to be done. All this was for the purpose of laying a foundation so that the gospel and His kingdom could be restored. Our mission today is to see that this gospel reaches every nation, every tongue, and every person. I repeat, this can be done effectively only when man's basic freedoms are protected and preserved. The gospel can prosper only in an atmosphere of freedom.

Today, there is a great threat to man's freedom. The Church is prospering and growing, but all over the world the light of freedom is being diminished. A great struggle for the minds of men is now being waged. At issue is whether or not man's basic inalienable rights of life, liberty, property, and pursuit of happiness shall be recognized. It is the same struggle over which the war in heaven was waged. In undiminished fury, and with an anxiety that his time is short—and it is—the great adversary to all men is attempting to destroy man's freedom and to see him totally subjugated. There are evidences of this struggle all about us. A system of slavery, communism, has imprisoned the minds and bodies of over one billion of the earth's inhabitants. Today, forty-five percent of the people of the world, in sixty-five nations, live under totalitarian dictatorships or forms of government that deny people most or all of their political and religious freedom. We further read and hear about international terrorism where nations are blackmailed and there is no regard for human life. Even among free nations we see the encroachment of government upon the lives of the citizenry by excessive taxation and regulation, all done under the guise that the people would not willfully or charitably distribute their wealth, so the government must take it from them. We further observe promises by the state of security, whereby men are taken care of from the womb to the tomb rather than earning this security by the "sweat of their brow"; deception in high places, with the justification that "the end justifies the means"; atheism; agnosticism; immorality; and dishonesty. The attendant results of such sin and usurpation of power lead to a general distrust of government officials; an insatiable, covetous spirit for more and more material wants; personal debt to satisfy this craving; and the disintegration of the family unit. Yes, we live today amidst the times the Savior spoke of, times when "the love of men shall wax cold, and iniquity shall abound."

In 1958 a beloved spiritual leader, and my inspired mission president in Great Britain, delivered an inspiring prayer at the dedication of the London Temple. I quote a short paragraph from that memorable prayer by President David O. McKay:

"Next to life we express gratitude for the gift of free agency. When thou didst create man, thou placed within him part of thine omnipotence and bade him choose for himself. Liberty and conscience thus became a sacred part of human nature. Freedom not only to think, but to speak and to act is a God-given privilege." (*Improvement Era,* October 1958, pp. 718-19.)

This heritage of freedom is as precious as life itself. It is truly a God-given gift to us. With it, we are moral agents before God, "accountable for [our] own sins in the day of judgment. Therefore, it is not right that any man should be in bondage one to another." (D&C 101:78-79.)

With the evidence all about them that tyranny is on the increase and that man's freedoms are ebbing, faithful members of the Church are asking, "What can be done? What can I do?" Of all people, members of the Church must not despair. As God has intervened in our past history, so He may in our present history. His purposes will not be thwarted. His kingdom will not be destroyed or left to another people, "but it shall break in pieces and consume all these kingdoms, and it shall stand for ever." (Daniel 2:44.) We must remember what our beloved President Spencer W. Kimball has reminded the Church so often: "Nothing is impossible to the Lord!"

To come under the protective and preserving hand of God, it is vital that we keep before us the conditions for such protection. "Righteousness exalteth a nation: but sin is a reproach to any people." (Proverbs 14:34.)

Nephi, who saw our day, pronounced this prophecy: ". . . I beheld that the church of the Lamb, who were the saints of God, were also upon all the face of the earth; and their dominions upon the face of the earth were small.

"And it came to pass that I, Nephi, beheld the power of the Lamb of God, that it descended upon the saints of the church of the Lamb, and upon the covenant people of the Lord, who were scattered upon all the face of the earth; *and they were armed with righteousness and with the power of God in great glory.*" (1 Nephi 14:12, 14. Italics added.)

And again, Nephi prophesied: "For the time soon cometh that the fulness of the wrath of God shall be poured out upon all the children of men; for he will not suffer that the wicked shall destroy the righteous. Wherefore, *he will preserve the righteous by his power,* even if it so be that the fulness of his wrath must come, and the righteous be preserved even unto the destruction of their enemies by fire." (1 Nephi 22:16-17. Italics added.)

These are the promises of the Lord to all the faithful saints who keep the commandments of God. They need not fear. What can we do to keep the light of freedom alive? Keep the commandments of

God. Walk circumspectly before Him. Pay our tithes and fast offerings. Attend our temples. Stay morally clean. Participate in local elections, for the Lord has said, "Honest men and wise men should be sought for diligently, and good men and wise men ye should observe to uphold." (D&C 98:10.) Be honest in all our dealings. Faithfully hold our family home evenings. Pray—pray to the God of heaven that He will intervene to preserve our precious freedoms, that His gospel may go to every nation and people. Yes, in the words of the Lord Himself: "Stand ye in holy places, and be not moved, until the day of the Lord come. . . ." (D&C 87:8.) Those "holy places" are our temples, stakes, wards, and homes.

At the time that the gospel was first taken to Great Britain in this dispensation, the elders were directed by the Spirit to go to Preston. A general election was in process. As the elders went into Preston, they were greeted with a spectacle of band and music playing, thousands of men, women, and children parading the streets, and flags flying in every direction. At the moment the coach in which the elders were riding had reached its destination, one of the flags was unfurled nearly over their heads. On the flag in large gilt letters was this motto: "Truth will prevail." The elders took this as an appropriate omen, and cried aloud, "Amen! Thanks be to God, truth *will* prevail!" I witness to you that certainty: truth will *prevail!*

God lives. He presides over the destiny of nations and His church. He is close to this church and its prophet. Of this I bear witness.

I love the British Isles and the British people. It was on that soil that I served my first mission. Since then I have had a great love for the people of the British Isles. When the first apostles set foot on that land, they were privileged to see Queen Victoria, who passed by them in royal procession. As she did so, she made a low bow to the brethren. They returned the royal salute, and Heber C. Kimball pronounced this blessing: "God bless you." As one of God's servants today, I say, God bless the people of the British Isles. God bless and preserve their families in righteousness. God bless their land and their leaders.

II

God's Hand in Our Nation's History

"Today we are almost engulfed by a tide of self-criticism, depreciation, and defamation of those who served our country honorably and with distinction. . . . When will we awaken to the fact that the defamation of our dead heroes only serves to undermine faith in the principles for which they stood and the institutions that they established?"

***

The destiny of America was divinely decreed. The events that established our great nation were foreknown to God and revealed to prophets of old. As in an enacted drama, the players who came on the scene were rehearsed and selected for their parts. Their talents, abilities, capacities, and weaknesses were known before they were born. As one looks back upon what we call our history, there is a telling theme that occurs again and again in this drama. It is, that God governs in the affairs of this nation. As the late President J. Reuben Clark, Jr., said, "This is the great motif which runs through our whole history."

A statement that President Harold B. Lee was fond of quoting was, "The frequent recurrence to fundamentals is essential to perpetuity." As one who is vitally concerned about the perpetuity of our liberties, our freedoms, and the principles laid down by the founders of this country, I refer to some fundamentals. To do so, I quote liberally from modern revelation, where we find this recurring theme repeatedly emphasized by those whom we uphold as prophets of God.

Unto the prophet Lehi, the Lord revealed: ". . . there shall none come into this land save they shall be brought by the hand of the Lord.

"Wherefore, this land is consecrated unto him whom he shall bring. And if it so be that they shall serve him according to the commandments which he hath given, it shall be a land of liberty unto them; wherefore, they shall never be brought down into captivity; if so, it shall be because of iniquity; for if iniquity shall abound cursed shall be the land for their sakes, but unto the righteous it shall be blessed forever." (2 Nephi 1:6-7.)

To the prophet Nephi the Lord said: "And inasmuch as ye shall keep my commandments, ye shall prosper, and shall be led to a land of promise; yea, even a land which I have prepared for you; yea, a land which is choice above all other lands." (1 Nephi 2:20.)

Nephi saw this in vision: "And I looked and beheld a man among the Gentiles, who was separated from the seed of my brethren by the many waters; *and I beheld the Spirit of God, that it came down and wrought upon the man;* and he went forth upon the many waters. . . ." (1 Nephi 13:12. Italics added.)

Though unnamed, this passage refers to Columbus. His own testimony about this epic voyage is recorded in a letter to the Spanish hierarchy and reads as follows: ". . . our Lord unlocked my mind, sent me upon the sea, and gave me fire for the deed. Those who heard of my emprise called it foolish, mocked me, and laughed. But who can doubt but that the Holy Ghost inspired me?" (Jacob Wassermann, *Columbus, Don Quixote of the Seas,* 1930, p. 20.)

Nephi continues: ". . . And I beheld the Spirit of the Lord, that it was upon the Gentiles, and they did prosper and obtain the land for their inheritance. . . . And it came to pass that I, Nephi, beheld that the Gentiles who had gone forth out of captivity did humble themselves before the Lord; *and the power of the Lord was with them.*" (1 Nephi 13:15-16. Italics added.)

This refers, of course, to the American colonists. Nephi then foresaw the great War of Independence: "And I beheld that their mother Gentiles were gathered together upon the waters, and upon the land also, to battle against them. And I beheld that *the power of God was with them,* and also that the wrath of God was upon all those that were gathered together against them to battle. And I, Nephi, beheld that the Gentiles that had gone out of captivity *were delivered by the power of God* out of the hands of all other nations." (1 Nephi 13:18-19. Italics added.)

All this was foreseen over 2300 years before it took place. Nephi's brother Jacob declared:

"But behold, this land, said God, shall be a land of thine inheritance, and the Gentiles shall be blessed upon the land.

"And this land shall be a land of liberty unto the Gentiles, and *there shall be no kings upon the land,* who shall raise up unto the Gentiles.

"And I will fortify this land against all other nations.

"And he that fighteth against Zion shall perish, saith God.

"For he that raiseth up a king against me shall perish, for I, the Lord, the king of heaven, will be their king, and I will be a light unto them forever, that hear my words." (2 Nephi 10:10-14. Italics added.)

America is a choice land, a land reserved for God's own purposes. America and its inhabitants are under an everlasting decree. The Lord revealed this decree to the brother of Jared:

"And now, we can behold the decrees of God concerning this land, that it is a land of promise; and whatsoever nation shall possess it shall serve God, or they shall be swept off when the fulness of his wrath shall come upon them. And the fulness of his wrath cometh upon them when they are ripened in iniquity.

"For behold, this is a land which is choice above all other lands; wherefore he that doth possess it shall serve God or shall be swept off; for it is the everlasting decree of God. And it is not until the fulness of iniquity among the children of the land, that they are swept off.

. . .

"Behold, this is a choice land, and whatsoever nation shall possess it shall be free from bondage, and from captivity, and from all other nations under heaven, if they will but serve the God of the land, who is Jesus Christ, who hath been manifested by the things which we have written." (Ether 2:9-12.)

Many great events have transpired in this land of destiny. This was the place where Adam dwelt; this was the place where the Garden of Eden was; it was here that Adam met with a body of high priests at Adam-ondi-Ahman shortly before his death and gave them his final blessing, and the place to which he will return to meet with the leaders of his people. This was the place of three former civilizations: that of Adam, that of the Jaredites, and that of the Nephites. This was also the place where our Heavenly Father and His Son, Jesus Christ, appeared to Joseph Smith, inaugurating the last dispensation.

The Lord has also decreed that this land should be "the place of the new Jerusalem, which should come down out of heaven, and the holy sanctuary of the Lord." (Ether 13:3.) Here is our nation's destiny! To serve God's eternal purposes and to prepare this land and people for America's eventual destiny, He "established the Constitution of this land, by the hands of wise men whom [He] raised up unto this very purpose, and redeemed the land by the shedding of blood." (D&C 101:80.)

No man, however brilliant and perceptive, shall have a complete perspective of our nation's history without this understanding and conviction. He must be persuaded by God's truth if he is to obtain a true and complete picture of our nation's origin and destiny. Secular scholarship, though useful, provides an incomplete and sometimes inaccurate view of our history. The real story of America is one that shows the hand of God in our nation's beginning. Why is it that this view of our history is almost lost in classrooms in America? Why is it that one must turn to the writers of the eighteenth and nineteenth centuries to find this view inferred or stated? The answer may perhaps be found in Abraham Lincoln's proclamation: "We have forgotten God. We have forgotten the gracious hand which preserved us in peace, and multiplied and enriched and strengthened us; and we have vainly imagined, in the deceitfulness of our hearts, that all these blessings were produced by some superior wisdom and virtue of our own. Intoxicated with unbroken success, we have become too self-sufficient to feel the necessity of redeeming and preserving grace, too proud to pray to the God that made us." (Abraham Lincoln, Proclamation for a National Fast Day, March 30, 1863.)

As a nation, we have become self-sufficient. This has given birth to a new religion in America that some have called secularism. This is a view of life without the idea that God is in the picture or that He had anything to do with the picture in the first place.

In the first century of our nation's history, the university was the guardian and preserver of faith in God. In this present century, the university has become ethically neutral, by and large agnostic. Our country is now reaping the effects of this agnostic influence. It has cost us an inestimable price. For who can place a price on the worth of a human soul, or the cost of the cynicism that young people have toward our republic and its leaders? I would have you consider soberly how this secular influence has affected the treatment of our nation's history in the textbook and classroom.

Today, students are subjected in their textbooks and classroom lectures to a subtle propaganda that there is a natural or rational explanation for all causes and events. Such a position removes the need for faith in God or belief in His interposition in the affairs of men. Events are *only*—and I purposely stress that word—explained from a humanistic frame of reference.

Historians and educational writers who are responsible for this movement are classified as "revisionists." Their purpose has been and is to create a "new history." By their own admission they are more influenced by their own training and other humanistic and scientific disciplines than any religious conviction. This detachment provides them, they say, with an objectivity that the older historians did not have. Many of the older historians, I should point out, were defenders of the patriots and their noble efforts. Feeling no obligation to perpetuate the ideals of the Founding Fathers, some of the "new historians" have cast a new body of beliefs for their secular faith. Their efforts, in some cases, have resulted in a new interpretation of our nation's history. May I illustrate a few of these reinterpretations.

First, that the American victory in the War of Independence was only the result of good fortune, ineptitude by the British generals, and the entrance of France into the war. All these facts are evident, but what is significantly left out are additional explanations that could provide the student with a spiritual perspective of our history. Why is it that we do not read in our history explanations such as this from George Washington: "The success, which has hitherto attended our united efforts, we owe to the gracious interposition of Heaven; and to that interposition let us gratefully ascribe the praise of victory, and the blessings of peace." (To the Executive of New Hampshire, November 3, 1789.)

Second, that the political thought of the Founding Fathers was the result of borrowed ideas from the eighteenth century philosophers. Again it is evident that the founders were men well schooled in the political thought of their times as well as ancient civilizations, but how does one account for the unity that came out of the impasse among the delegates at the Constitutional Convention? It was at that point that Benjamin Franklin made his great speech. He solemnly counseled:

"I have lived, Sir, a long time; and the longer I live, the more convincing proofs I see of this truth, that God governs in the affairs of men. And, if a sparrow cannot fall to the ground without his notice, is it probable that an empire can rise without his aid? We have been assured, Sir, in the Sacred Writings, that 'except the Lord build the house, they labor in vain that build it.' I firmly believe this; and I also believe, that, without his concurring aid, we shall succeed in this political building no better than the builders of Babel; we shall be divided by our little, partial, local interests, our projects will be confounded, and we ourselves shall become a reproach and a by-word down to future ages. And, what is worse, mankind may hereafter, from this unfortunate instance, despair of establishing governments by human wisdom, and leave it to chance, war, and conquest.

"I therefore beg leave to move,

"That henceforth prayers, imploring the assistance of Heaven, and its blessings on our deliberations, be held in this assembly every morning before we proceed to business; and that one or more of the clergy of this city be requested to officiate in that service." (Jared Sparks, *The Works of Benjamin Franklin,* 1837, pp. 155-56.)

Some historians have ignored this dimension because Madison, who reported the Constitutional Convention, said nothing about it.

Others report that the motion was not acted on. Another member of the convention, Jonathan Dayton of New Jersey, who also reported it, said the motion was acted on favorably by the convention.

Again, I would ask: Why is it that the references to God's influence in the noble efforts of the founders of our republic are not mentioned? Listen to the convictions of two of these delegates to the Constitutional Convention. First, Charles Pinckney: ". . . When the great work was done and published, I was . . . struck with amazement. Nothing less than that superintending hand of Providence, that so miraculously carried us through the war . . . , could have brought it about so complete, upon the whole." (P. L. Ford, ed., *Essays on the Constitution,* 1892, p. 412.)

The other testimony is from James Madison, sometimes referred to as the "Father of the Constitution": "It is impossible for the man of pious reflection not to perceive in it a finger of that Almighty hand which has been so frequently and signally extended to our relief in the critical stages of the revolution." (*Federalist,* no. 37.)

Third, the charge that the founders designed the Constitution primarily to benefit themselves and their class (property owners) financially, and that the economic motif was their dominant incentive. Such was the thesis of the American historian, Dr. Charles Beard. Yet Madison said: "There was never an assembly of men . . . who were more pure in their motives." We must remember that these were men who had sacrificed in many cases their fortunes and their sacred honor.

Shortly after the turn of this century, Charles Beard published his work *An Economic Interpretation of the Constitution of the United States.* This book marked the beginning of a trend to defame the motives and integrity of the founders of the Constitution. It also grossly distorted the real intent of the founders by suggesting their motivation was determined by economics—a thesis that had originated with Karl Marx. Beard himself was not a Marxist, but he was socialist in his thinking and he admitted there was much we could learn from Marx's ideas. Before his death Beard recanted his own thesis, but the damage had been done. This began a new trend in educational and intellectual circles in the United States.

Not infrequently this penchant for historical criticism has resulted in the defamation of character of the Founding Fathers. It is done under the guise of removing the so-called myths that surround their background. A favorite target of this defamation has been George Washington, our nation's most illustrious leader. Some of these so-called new historians have questioned his honesty, challenged his military leadership and executive ability, and impugned his moral character.

Others who have taken measure of the man have assessed matters differently. John Lord, author of the well-known work of the nineteenth century, *Beacon Lights of History*, wrote this of Washington: "Washington . . . had a transcendent character. . . . As a man he had his faults, but they were so few and so small that they seemed to be but spots upon a sun. These have been forgotten; and as the ages roll on mankind will see naught but the lustre of his virtues and the greatness of his services." (New York, 1894, 7:168.)

Winston Churchill estimated Washington thus: "George Washington holds one of the proudest titles that history can bestow. He was the Father of his Nation. Almost alone his staunchness in the War of Independence held the American colonies to their united purpose. . . . He filled his office with dignity and inspired his administration with much of his own wisdom. To his terms as President are due the smooth organisation of the Federation Government, the establishment of national credit, and the foundation of a foreign policy." (*A History of the English Speaking People: The Age of Revolution,* New York: Dodd, Mead, and Co., 1967, p. 347.)

William H. Wilbur, author of the commendable little volume *The Making of George Washington,* made this appraisal:

"Greatness of moral character, forthright honesty, quiet modesty, thoughtful consideration for others, thoroughness, kindness, and generosity! During the American Revolution, and for more than fifty years thereafter, young Americans were inspired to attain these qualities by the vivid recollections of men who had served with George Washington, men who knew him from intimate daily association. As years went by, books, stories, living personal memories, all combined to present this great hero in such a way as to make him an inspiring and potent influence for good. . . .

"Unfortunately the last seventy-five years have produced a marked change. In these years it has come to be standard practice for Washington authors to proclaim it as their purpose to 'humanize' the Washington image. Most of them have instead succeeded in belittling him. They have replaced a glorious, inspiring memory with a tawdry, warped picture." (*The Making of George Washington,* 1970, pp. 19, 21.)

Elder Mark E. Petersen has recently written a remarkable little book, *The Great Prologue.* It provides the prophetic history of our nation's history and its founders. Within that volume, Elder Petersen assesses Washington's character in these words:

"In many respects [Washington] was like Moroni, the noted general of the Book of Mormon, who . . . hoisted his banner of liberty.

"Washington was the personification of honesty, even as Lincoln, with whom he became a supreme example of integrity in public office. He had the true vision of one united nation of separate states, with an inspired Constitution to give strength to the whole, but with liberty assured to the several units." (Deseret Book, 1975, pp. 90-91.)

And lest these testimonies are not convincing, President Wilford Woodruff said of the Founding Fathers collectively, and of Washington specifically:

"I am going to bear my testimony . . . that those men who laid the foundation of this American government . . . were the *best spirits* the God of heaven could find on the face of the earth. They were choice spirits, *not wicked men.* General Washington and all the men that labored for the purpose were inspired of the Lord. . . .

"Every one of those men that signed the Declaration of Independence, with General Washington, called upon me, as an Apostle of the Lord Jesus Christ, in the Temple at St. George, two consecutive nights, and demanded at my hands that I should go forth and attend to the ordinances of the House of God for them. . . . Brother McAllister baptized me for all those men, and then I told those brethren that it was their duty to go into the Temple and labor until they had got endowments for all of them. They did it. Would those spirits have called upon me, as an Elder in Israel, to perform that work if they had not been noble spirits before God? They would not." (*Conference Report,* April 1898, pp. 89-90.)

The temple work for the fifty-six signers of the Declaration of Independence and other Founding Fathers has been done. All these appeared to Wilford Woodruff when he was president of the St. George Temple. President George Washington was ordained a high priest at that time. You will also be interested to know that, according to Wilford Woodruff's journal, John Wesley, Benjamin Franklin, and Christopher Columbus were also ordained high priests at that time. When one casts doubt about the character of these noble sons of God, I believe he or she will have to answer to the God of heaven for it. Yes, with Lincoln I say: "To add brightness to the sun or glory to the name of Washington is . . . impossible. Let none attempt it. In solemn awe pronounce the name and in its naked deathless splendor, leave it shining on."

If ever this country needed the timeless wisdom of the father of our country, it is today. How much our country could benefit by following the wisdom of our country's first president. Here are a few among many maxims:

"Let the reins of government then be braced and held with a steady hand, and every violation of the constitution be reprehended. If defective, let it be amended, but not suffered to be trampled upon whilst it has an existence." (To Henry Lee, October 31, 1786, *Writings* 29:34.)

"To be prepared for war is one of the most effectual means of preserving peace." (First Annual Address, January 8, 1790, *Writings* 12:8.)

". . . the love of my country will be the ruling influence of my conduct." (Answer to the New Hampshire Executive, November 3, 1789, *Writings* 12:175.)

". . . a good moral character is the first essential in a man. . . . It is therefore highly important, that you should endeavor not only to be learned, but virtuous." (To George Steptoe Washington, December 5, 1790, *Writings* 10:123-24.)

"Let us unite, therefore, in imploring the Supreme Ruler of nations to spread his holy protection over these United States; to turn the machinations of the wicked to the confirming of our constitution; to enable us at all times to root out internal sedition, and put invasion to flight; to perpetuate to our country that prosperity, which his goodness has already conferred; and to verify the anticipations of this government being a safeguard to human rights." (To the Senate and House of Representatives, November 19, 1794, *Writings* 12:54.)

It would profit all of us as citizens to read again Washington's Farewell Address to his countrymen. The address is prophetic. I believe it ranks alongside the Declaration of Independence and the Constitution.

My feelings about this tendency to discredit our Founding Fathers are well summarized by the late President J. Reuben Clark, Jr., in these words: "These were the horse and buggy days as they have been called in derision; these were the men who traveled in the horse-drawn buggies and on horseback; but these were the men who carried under their hats, as they rode in the buggies and on their horses, a political wisdom garnered from the ages. As giants to pygmies are they when placed alongside our political emigres and their fellow travelers of today, who now traduce them with slighting word and contemptuous phrase." (*Stand Fast by Our Constitution*, pp. 136-37.)

Today we are almost engulfed by this tide of self-criticism, depreciation, and defamation of those who served our country honorably and with distinction. A most recent victim of the tarnish brush is J.

Edgar Hoover. I knew Mr. Hoover personally. He was a God-fearing man, and one of the most honorable and able men I have known in government service. By innuendo, lesser men, whose own motives are questionable, have maligned his motives and good character.

I know the philosophy behind this practice—"to tell it as it is." All too often those who subscribe to this philosophy are not hampered by too many facts. When will we awaken to the fact that the defamation of our dead heroes only serves to undermine faith in the principles for which they stood and the institutions that they established? Some have termed this practice as "historical realism" or moderately called it "debunking." I call it slander and defamation. And I repeat, those who are guilty of it in their writing or teaching will answer to a higher tribunal.

We should not, therefore, be astonished when other nations view the United States as a "faltering democracy." How long would a basketball team that was ranked number one in the polls remain in that position if the student body, the school paper, and supporting faculty constantly pointed out its weaknesses? Soon the team would begin to lack confidence and fail. This is what we have been doing in our blessed country. Our heroes and institutions have been tarnished. We are constantly being reminded, via the press and other media, of what is wrong in our country. A recent editorial in the London *Daily Telegraph* appealed to us:

"The United States should know that her European cousins and allies are appalled and disgusted by the present open disarray of her public life. The self-criticism and self-destructive tendencies are running mad, with no countervailing force in sight. . . . Please, America, for God's sake pull yourself together." (As quoted in *U.S. News and World Report,* January 26, 1976, p. 88.)

It is the job of the historian and educator and church leader to help us as a nation to pull ourselves together, to help us regain perspective and vision and the respect of all nations. This will not be done by showing that this is merely a phase through which we are passing. No, it will be done by men who possess a love of country, a vision of our country's future, and the assurance of her divinely guided destiny.

This humanistic emphasis on history is not confined only to secular history. There have been and continue to be attempts to bring this philosophy into our own Church history. Again the emphasis is to underplay revelation and God's intervention in significant events, and to inordinately humanize the prophets of God so that their human frailties become more apparent than their spiritual qualities. It is a state of mind and spirit characterized by one history buff who asked: "Do you believe the Church has arrived at a sufficient state of maturity where we can begin to tell our *real* story?" Inferred in that question is the accusation that the Church has not been telling the truth. Unfortunately, too many of those who have been intellectually gifted become so imbued with criticism that they become disaffected spiritually.

Some of these have attempted to reinterpret Joseph Smith and his revelations. They offer what they call a psychological interpretation of his motives and actions. This interpretation suggests that whether or not Joseph Smith actually saw God the Father and His Son, Jesus Christ, or other visions is really unimportant. What matters is that he *thought* he did. To those who have not sought after or received a testimony of Joseph Smith's divine calling, he will ever remain what one called "the enigma from Palmyra."

I recall the prophetic pronouncement made by President George Albert Smith when one of our own apostatized and wrote a biography about the Prophet Joseph Smith. President Smith made this statement before the general conference of the Church: "There have been some who have belittled [Joseph Smith], but I would like to say that those who have done so will be forgotten and their remains will go back to mother earth, . . . and the odor of their infamy will never die, while the glory and honor and majesty and courage and fidelity manifested by the Prophet Joseph Smith will attach to his name forever." (*Conference Report,* April 1946, p. 182.)

No writer can ever accurately portray a prophet of God if he or she does not believe in prophecy. They cannot succeed in writing what they do not have in personal faith. That is why the best biography on Joseph Smith to date was one done by one who knew him and who served the Church as an apostle and member of the First Presidency. I refer to George Q. Cannon's inspiring work, *The Life of Joseph Smith.*

Another prophet whom some historians like to humanize is Brigham Young. One writer accused him of being "an accessory after the fact" to the infamous Mountain Meadows massacre incident. He is sometimes referred to as an autocrat. Another fictionalized version of him is that he was continually groping for a revelation that never came to him. Among many testimonies to the contrary are these. Brigham Young himself declared:

"God *has shown me* that this is the spot to locate His people. . . . We shall build a city and a temple to the Most High God in this place. We will extend our settlements to the east and west, to the north and to the south, and we will build towns and cities by the hundreds, and thousands of the Saints will gather in from the nations of the earth. This will become the great highway of the nations. Kings and emperors and the noble and wise of the earth will visit us here. . . ." (James S. Brown, *Life of a Pioneer,* 1900, pp. 121-22. Italics added.)

Wilford Woodruff said that Brigham Young saw the Salt Lake Valley "in vision . . . and . . . the future glory of Zion and of Israel, as they would be, planted in the valleys of these mountains." (*Journal History,* July 24, 1880.)

More recently one of our Church educators published what he purports to be a history of the Church's stand on the question of organic evolution. His thesis challenges the integrity of a prophet of God. He suggests that Joseph Fielding Smith published his work *Man: His Origin and Destiny* against the counsel of the First Presidency and his own brethren. This writer's interpretation is not only inaccurate, but it runs counter to the testimony of Elder Mark E. Petersen, who wrote this foreword to President Smith's book, a book I would encourage all of you to read:

"Some of us [members of the Council of the Twelve] urged [Elder Joseph Fielding Smith] to write a book on the creation of the world and the origin of man. . . . The present volume is the result. It is a most remarkable presentation of material from both sources [science and religion] under discussion. It will fill a great need in the Church, and will be particularly invaluable to students who have become confused by the misapplication of information derived from scientific experimentation." (Foreword, *Man: His Origin and Destiny,* Deseret Book Co., 1954.)

When one understands that the author to whom I allude is an exponent for the theory of organic evolution, his motive in disparaging President Joseph Fielding Smith becomes apparent. To hold to a private opinion on such matters is one thing, but when one undertakes to publish his views to discredit the work of a prophet, it is a very serious matter. It is also apparent to all who have the Spirit of God in them that Joseph Fielding Smith's writings will stand the test of time.

Lest there be some who get the impression that I am an antagonist to the discipline of history and historians, let me declare my feelings about that noble profession. I love to read history and historical biography. I have great respect for the historian who can put into proper perspective events and people, and make history come alive. I believe the maxim that "those who do not understand the lessons of the past are doomed to repeat those errors anew." I love history books that tell history as it was—as the Book of Mormon tells it—with God in the picture guiding and directing the affairs of the righteous. I love to read history for its timeless lessons and for the inspiration I can gather from the lives of great leaders. I have been privileged to know many in my lifetime who have made history both in the world scene and in the Church.

My purpose is to help you to discern a trend that has been destructive to the faith of many of our people in our nation's founders and in our country's divine origin and destiny. My purpose further is to forewarn you about a humanistic emphasis that would tarnish our own Church history and its leaders.

My plea to you is to stir up the gift that is within you. You will recall the Lord told us why we needed to exercise the spiritual gifts He has given us: ". . . beware lest ye are deceived; and that ye may not be deceived seek ye earnestly the best gifts. . . ." (D&C 46:8.) If there was ever the need to apply that counsel, it is now. Those gifts of the spirit are needed to discern truth from error.

I bear witness that America's history was foreknown to God; that His divine intervention and merciful providence has given us both peace and prosperity in this beloved land; that through His omiscience and benevolent design He selected and sent some of His choicest spirits to lay the foundation of our government. These men were inspired of God to do the work they accomplished. They were not evil men. Their work was a prologue to the restoration of the gospel and the Church of Jesus Christ. It was done in fulfillment of the ancient prophets who declared that this was a promised land, "a land of liberty unto the Gentiles," and that is us.

I testify that God, our Heavenly Father, and His Son, Jesus Christ, have visited this land. They appeared in the state of New York to Joseph Smith, Jr. I testify that their appearance was a reality. Since that time the work of God has moved forward under the inspired leadership and prophetic direction of Joseph Smith, Brigham Young, John Taylor, Wilford Woodruff, Lorenzo Snow, Joseph F. Smith, Heber J. Grant, George Albert Smith, David O. McKay, Joseph Fielding Smith, Harold B. Lee, and our prophet today, Spencer W. Kimball.

This is the kingdom that Daniel of old saw in vision, a kingdom "which shall never be destroyed: and . . . shall not be left to other people." (Daniel 2:44.) This church and kingdom is on course in fulfilling its prophetic destiny.

I testify that this is the Lord's church. He presides over it and is close to His servants. He is not an absentee master, of that you can be assured.

Yes, we are privileged to live in a choice land—a land of Zion—a land reserved for the second coming of our Lord and Savior, and the Lord's base of operations today. When all these events are finished and written, we will look back and not be astonished to see that the prophecies, ancient and modern, about this land and these events were but our history in reverse. For that is what prophecy is.

May God bless us all to be faithful and true to this vision, and to uphold, sustain, and defend this nation, its founders, and the kingdom of God.

III

The Signers of the Declaration of Independence

"I thank God for the sacrifices and efforts made by our Founding Fathers, whose efforts brought us the blessings we have today. Their lives should be reminders to us that we are the blessed beneficiaries of a liberty earned by great sacrifice of property, reputation, and life."

As we read the newspapers and other printed materials, listen to television and radio, and read or hear the voices of distinguished Americans, we become conscious that America is at the crossroads. We stand today with the reality before us that we could lose our great heritage of freedom.

There are those in our midst who depreciate our great beloved republic and the men who laid the foundation of our government. These are the voices and the words that our youth frequently hear or read. I ask, How can they be expected to feel a duty to God and their country when the climate of opinion is so negative to all that we cherish and hold dear? The answer to that question will be decided by how well our homes instill a love of God and of our country and how well we as leaders exemplify before our youth our devotion. When was the last time you took the occasion to let them know your feelings about your country?

This nation is unlike any other nation. It was uniquely born. It had its beginning when fifty-six men affixed their signatures to the Declaration of Independence. I realize there are some who view that declaration as only a political document. It is much more than that. It constitutes a spiritual manifesto, declaring not for this nation alone, but for all nations, the source of man's rights.

The purpose of the declaration was to set forth the moral justifications of a rebellion against a long-recognized political tradition—the divine right of kings. At issue was the fundamental question of whether men's rights were God-given or whether these rights were to be dispensed by governments to their subjects. This document proclaimed that all men have certain inalienable rights; in other words, that those rights came from God. The colonists were therefore not rebels against political authority. Their contention was not with

Parliament nor the British people; it was against a tyrannical monarch who had "conspired," "incited," and "plundered" them. They were thus morally justified to revolt, for as it was stated in the declaration, "when a long train of abuses and usurpations, pursuing invariably the same Object, evinces a design to reduce them under absolute Despotism, it is their right, it is their duty, to throw off such Government, and to provide new Guards for their future security."

The document concludes with this pledge: "For the support of this Declaration, with a firm reliance on the Protection of Divine Providence, we mutually pledge to each other our Lives, our Fortunes, and our sacred Honor."

How prophetic that pledge was to be! Consider with me some of the sacrifices made by these signers.

Fifty-six men signed the document on August 2, 1776, or in the case of some, shortly thereafter. They came from all walks of life. Twenty-three were lawyers, twelve were merchants, twelve were men of the soil, four were physicians, two were manufacturers, one was a politician, one a printer, and another a minister.

Almost a third of the signers were under forty years of age; eighteen were in their thirties and three in their twenties. Only seven were over sixty. The youngest, Edward Rutledge of South Carolina, was twenty-six and a half, and the oldest, Benjamin Franklin, was seventy. Three of the signers lived to be over ninety. Charles Carroll died at age ninety-five. Ten died in their eighties.

Possibly as many as six of the signers were childless in their marriages (two never did marry), but the remainder sired 325 children. Carter Braxton had 18 children; William Ellery, 17; and Robert Sherman, 15.

The signers were religious men, all being Protestant except Charles Carroll, who was Roman Catholic. Over half expressed their religious faith as being Episcopalian. Others were Congregational, Presbyterian, Quaker, and Baptist.

Two of the signers would become presidents of the United States—Thomas Jefferson, the author of the declaration, and John Adams. Two—John Adams and Benjamin Harrison—would be fathers of future presidents. Another, Elbridge Gerry, was the vice-president under James Madison.

Those signers pledged their lives, and some paid that price for this nation's birth—and our birthright.

At least nine of them died as a result of the war or its hardships on them. The first of the signers to die was John Morton of Pennsylvania. He was at first sympathetic to the British, but finally changed his mind and cast his vote for independence. By doing so, his friends, relatives, and neighbors turned against him. Those who knew him best said this ostracism hastened his death, for he lived only eight months after the signing. His last words were, ". . . tell them that they will live to see the hour when they shall acknowledge it to have been the most glorious service that I ever rendered to my country."

Another to pay with his life was Caesar Rodney. Suffering facial cancer, he left his sickbed at midnight and rode all night by horseback through a severe storm. He arrived just in time to cast the deciding vote for his delegation in favor of independence. His doctors told him he needed treatment obtainable only in Europe. He refused to go in this time of his country's crisis. The decision cost him his life.

When the British came to Trenton, they settled near the home of John Hart, one of the five signers from New Jersey. He had a large farm and several grist mills. While his wife was on her deathbed, Hessian soldiers descended on Hart's property. They destroyed his mills, ravaged his property, and scattered his thirteen children. Hart became a hunted fugitive. When he finally returned to his land, he was broken in health, his farmland was scourged, his wife had died, and his children were all scattered. He died three years after signing the declaration.

Yes, the signers also pledged their fortunes, and at least fifteen saw the realization of that pledge. Twelve had their homes ransacked or ruined. Six literally gave their fortunes to further the cause. When the four New York delegates signed the declaration, they signed away their property. William Floyd was exiled from his home for seven years and was practically ruined financially. Francis Lewis had his home plundered and burned, and his wife was carried away prisoner. She suffered great brutality and never regained her health; she died within two years. He never regained his fortune. Robert Morris had his property destroyed and, like Floyd, was denied his home for seven years. Phillip Livingston never saw his home again, for his estate became a British naval hospital. He sold all of his remaining property to finance the revolution. He died before the war was over.

Another signer, merchant Robert Morris, lost 150 ships, which were sunk during the war. Three of the four signers from South Carolina—Thomas Heyward, Arthur Middleton, and Edward Rutledge—were taken prisoner by the British and imprisoned for ten months.

Thomas Nelson, Jr., of Virginia died in poverty at age fifty-one. He gave his fortune to help finance the war and never regained either it or his health. Before Patrick Henry gave his great speech, he was preceded by Nelson who said, "I am a merchant of Yorktown, but I am a Virginian first. Let my trade perish. I call God to witness that if any British troops are landed in the County of Yorks, of which I am a Lieutenant, I will wait no order, but will summon the militia and drive the invaders into the sea."

When Patrick Henry declared his immortal words, ". . . give me liberty or give me death," he was not speaking idly. When those signers affixed their signatures to that sacred document, they were, in a real sense, choosing liberty or death, for if the revolution failed, if their fight had come to naught, they would be hanged as traitors.

Yes, the signers fulfilled their pledge. Their spirit of sacrifice was exemplified by John Adams, who, when others were vacillating on whether to adopt the declaration, declared:

"Sink or swim, live or die, survive or perish, I give my hand and my heart to this vote. It is true, indeed, that in the beginning we aimed not at independence. But there's a Divinity which shapes our ends. . . . Why, then, should we defer the Declaration? . . .

". . . You and I, indeed, may rue it. We may not live to the time when this Declaration shall be made good. We may die; die colonists; die slaves; die, it may be, ignominiously and on the scaffold. Be it so, Be it so. If it be the pleasure of Heaven that my country shall require the poor offering of my life, the victim shall be ready. . . . But while I do live, let me have a country, or at least the hope of a country, and that a free country.

"But whatever may be our fate, be assured . . . that this Declaration will stand. It may cost treasure, and it may cost blood; but it will stand, and it will richly compensate for both. Through the thick gloom of the present, I see the brightness of the future, as the sun in heaven. We shall make this a glorious, an immortal day. When we are in our graves, our children will honor it. They will celebrate it with thanksgiving, with festivity, with bonfires, and illuminations. On its annual return they will shed tears, copious, gushing tears, not of subjection and slavery, not of agony and distress, but of exultation, of gratitude, and of joy. Sir, before God, I believe the hour is come. My judgment approves this measure, and my whole heart is in it. All that I have, and all that I am, and all that I hope, in this life, I am now ready here to stake upon it; and I leave off as I begun, that live or die, survive or perish, I am for the Declaration. It is my living sentiment, and by the blessing of God it shall be my dying sentiment, Independence, now, and Independence for ever." (*The Works of Daniel Webster,* 4th ed., 1851, 1:133-36.)

How fitting it is that we sing in "America the Beautiful":
> "O beautiful for heroes proved
>   In liberating strife,
> Who more than self their country loved,
>   And mercy more than life!"

These patriots were willing to make the effort and sacrifice they did because they understood a fundamental that seems to be forgotten today: that the rights of man are either God-given as part of a divine plan or they are granted as part of a political plan. Reason, necessity, and religious conviction and belief in the sovereignty of God led these men to accept the divine origin of man's rights. To God's glory, and the credit of these men, our nation had its unique birth.

If we accept the premise that human rights are granted by government, then we must be willing to accept the corollary that they can be denied by government. If Americans should ever come to believe that their rights and freedoms are instituted among men by politicians and bureaucrats, then they will no longer carry the proud inheritance of their forefathers, but will grovel before their masters seeking favors and dispensations—a throwback to the feudal system of the Dark Ages. We must ever keep in mind the inspired words of Thomas Jefferson, as found in the Declaration of Independence:

"We hold these truths to be self-evident, that all men are created equal; that they are endowed by their Creator with certain unalienable Rights, that among these are Life, Liberty, and the pursuit of Happiness. That to secure these rights, Governments are instituted among Men, deriving their just powers from the consent of the governed."

Since God created man with certain inalienable rights, and man, in turn, created government to help secure and safeguard those rights, it follows that man is superior to government and should remain master over it, not the other way around. As said so appropriately by Lord Acton:

"It was from America that the plain ideas that men ought to mind their own business, and that the nation is responsible to Heaven for the acts of the State,—ideas long locked in the breast of solitary thinkers, and hidden among Latin folios,—burst forth like a conqueror upon the world they were destined to transform, under the title of the Rights of Man. . . .

". . . and the principle gained ground, that a nation can never abandon its fate to an authority it cannot control." (*The History of Freedom and Other Essays,* 1907, pp. 55-56.)

We also need to keep before us the truth that people who do not master themselves and their appetites will soon be mastered by government.

I wonder if we are not rearing a generation that seemingly does not understand this fundamental principle. Yet this is the principle that separates our country from all others. The central issue before the people today is the same issue that inflamed the hearts of our Founding Fathers in 1776 to strike out for independence. That issue is whether the individual exists for the state or whether the state exists for the individual.

In a republic, the real danger is that we may slowly slide into a condition of slavery of the individual to the state rather than entering this condition by a sudden revolution. The loss of our liberties might easily come about, not through the ballot box, but through the abandonment of the fundamental teachings from God and this basic principle upon which our country was founded. Such a condition is usually brought about by a series of little steps which, at the time, seem justified by a variety of reasons.

Yes, I thank God for the sacrifices and efforts made by our Founding Fathers, whose efforts brought us the blessings we have today. Their lives should be reminders to us that we are blessed beneficiaries of a liberty earned by great sacrifice of property, reputation, and life. There should be no doubt what our task is today. If we truly cherish the freedoms we have, we must instill these sacred principles in the hearts and minds of our youth. We have the obligation to rekindle the flame that existed two hundred years ago among those who pledged their lives, their fortunes, and their sacred honor. The opportunity for patriots to do so again is clearly upon us.

IV

The Constitution:
A Glorious Standard

"Unless we as citizens of this nation forsake our sins, political and otherwise, and return to the fundamental principles of Christianity and of constitutional government, we will lose our political liberties, our free institutions, and will stand in jeopardy before God of losing our exaltation."

Every Latter-day Saint should love the inspired Constitution of the United States—a nation with a spiritual foundation and a prophetic history, which nation the Lord has declared to be his base of operations in these latter days. The framers of the Constitution were men raised up by God to establish this foundation of our government, for so the Lord has declared by revelation in these words: "I established the Constitution of this land, by the hands of wise men whom I raised up unto this very purpose, and redeemed the land by the shedding of blood." (D&C 101:80.)

Yes, this is a land fertilized by the blood of patriots. During the struggle for independence, nearly 9,000 of the colonist forces were killed. Among those fifty-six patriots who had pledged their lives, their fortunes, and their sacred honor by signing the Declaration of Independence, at least nine paid that price with their life's blood.

At the close of the revolution, the thirteen states found themselves independent, but they then faced internal economic and political problems. The Articles of Confederation had been adopted but proved to be ineffectual. Under this instrument, the nation was without a president, a head. There was a congress, but it was a body destitute of any power. There was no supreme court. The states were merely a confederation.

Washington wrote of the defects of this loose federation in these words: "The fabrick which took nine years, at the expense of much blood and treasure to rear, now totters to the foundation, and without support must soon fall." (*Writings of George Washington,* U.S. Government Printing Office, 1939, 29:68.) Because of this crisis, fifty-five of the seventy-four appointed delegates reported to the convention, representing every state except Rhode Island, for the purpose of forming "a more perfect union." Thirty-nine finally signed the Constitution.

Who were these delegates, those whom the Lord raised up and designated "wise men"? They were mostly young men in the prime of life, their average age being forty-four. Benjamin Franklin was the eldest at eighty-one. George Washington, the presiding officer of the convention, was fifty-five. Alexander Hamilton was only thirty-two; James Madison, who recorded the proceedings of the convention with his remarkable *Notes,* was thirty-six. These were young men, but men of exceptional character, "sober, seasoned, distinguished men of affairs, drawn from various walks of life." (J. Reuben Clark, Jr., *Stand Fast by Our Constitution,* p. 135.)

Of the thirty-nine signers, twenty-one were educated in the leading American colleges and in Great Britain; eighteen were, or had been, lawyers or judges; twenty-six had seen service in the Continental Congress; nineteen had served in the Revolutionary army, seventeen as officers; four had been on Washington's personal staff during the war. Among that assembly of the thirty-nine signers were to be found two future presidents of the United States, one the "father of his country"; a vice-president of the United States; a Secretary of the Treasury; a Secretary of War; a Secretary of State; two chief justices of the Supreme Court, and three who served as justices; and the venerable Franklin, diplomat, philosopher, scientist, and statesman.

"They were not backwoodsmen from the far-off frontiers, not one of them. . . . There has not been another such group of men in all the [200] years of our history, no group that even challenged the supremacy of this group." (J. Reuben Clark, Jr., *Conference Report,* April 1957, p. 47.) President Wilford Woodruff said they "were the best spirits the God of heaven could find on the face of the earth. They were choice spirits. . . ." (*Conference Report,* April 1898, p. 89.)

Following the drafting, the Constitution awaited ratification by the states. In 1787 three states ratified it. In the next year eight more followed; and on April 6, 1789, the Constitution of the United States went into operation as the basic law of the United States when the electoral college unanimously elected George Washington as the first president of the nation. This date, I believe, was not accidental.

In the final analysis, what the framers did, under the inspiration of God, was to draft a document that merited the approval of God Himself, who declared it to "be maintained for the rights and protection of all flesh." (D&C 101:77.)

The document has been criticized by some as outmoded, and even a recent president of the United States criticized it as a document "written for an entirely different period of our nation's history." (*U.S. News and World Report,* December 17, 1962, p. 104.) The eminent constitutional authority, J. Reuben Clark, Jr., has answered this argument in these words: "These were the horse and buggy days as they have been called in derision; these were the men who traveled in the horsedrawn buggies and on horseback; but these were the men who carried under their hats, as they rode in the buggies and on their horses, a political wisdom garnered from the ages." (*Stand Fast by Our Constitution,* p. 136.)

What those framers did can be better appreciated when it is considered that when the instrument went into operation, it covered only thirteen states with fewer than four million people. Today it adequately covers fifty states and over 200 million people.

The wisdom of those delegates is shown in the genius of the document itself. The founders had a strong distrust for centralized power in the federal government, so they created a government with checks and balances. This was to prevent any branch of the government from becoming too powerful.

Congress could pass laws, but the president could check this with a veto. Congress, however, could override the veto and, by its means of initiative in taxation, could further restrain the executive department. The Supreme Court could nullify laws passed by the Congress and signed by the president, but Congress could limit the court's appellate jurisdiction. The president could appoint judges for their lifetime with the consent of the Senate.

Each branch of the government was also made subject to different political pressures. The president was to be chosen by electors, senators by state legislatures, representatives by the people, and the Supreme Court by the president, with the consent of the Senate.

All this was deliberately designed to make it difficult for a majority of the people to control the government and to place restraint on the government itself. The founders created a republic which Jefferson described as "action by the citizens in person in affairs within their reach and competence, and in all others by representatives. . . ." (*Works of Thomas Jefferson,* 1905, 11:523.) A study of the principles that undergird the document would be profitable for all Americans.

When James Russell Lowell was asked, "How long will the American Republic endure?" he replied: "As long as the ideas of the men who founded it continue dominant." May I comment on one of the most vital ideas and principles.

Constitutional government, as designed by the framers, will survive only with a righteous people. "Our constitution," said John Adams (first vice-president and second president), "was made only for a moral and religious people. It is wholly inadequate to the government of any other." (John R. Howe, Jr., *The Changing Political Thought of John Adams,* Princeton University Press, 1966, p. 185.)

America, North and South, is a choice land, a land reserved for God's own purposes. This land and its inhabitants are under an everlasting decree. The Lord revealed this decree to the brother of Jared, an American prophet, in these solemn words:

"And now, we can behold the decrees of God concerning this land, that it is a land of promise; and whatsoever nation shall possess it shall serve God, or they shall be swept off when the fulness of his wrath shall come upon them. And the fulness of his wrath cometh upon them when they are ripened in iniquity.

"For behold, this is a land which is choice above all other lands; wherefore he that doth possess it shall serve God or shall be swept off; for it is the everlasting decree of God. . . .

"Behold, this is a choice land, and whatsoever nation shall possess it shall be free from bondage, and from captivity, and from all other nations under heaven, if they will but serve the God of the land, who is Jesus Christ. . . ." (Ether 2:9-12.)

The Lord has also decreed that this land should be "the place of the New Jerusalem, which should come down out of heaven, and the holy sanctuary of the Lord." (Ether 13:3.) Here is our nation's destiny! To serve God's eternal purposes and to prepare this land and people for America's eventual destiny, the Lord established the Constitution of this land by the hands of wise men whom He raised up to this very purpose.

Many Americans have lost sight of the truth that righteousness is the one indispensable ingredient to liberty. Perhaps as never before in our history is our nation collectively deserving of the indictment pronounced by Abraham Lincoln in these words:

"We have been the recipients of the choicest bounties of Heaven. We have been preserved, these many years, in peace and prosperity. We have grown in numbers, wealth, and power as no other nation has ever grown; but we have forgotten God. We have forgotten the gracious hand which preserved us in peace, and multiplied and enriched and strengthened us; and we have vainly imagined, in the deceitfulness of our hearts, that all these blessings were produced by some superior wisdom and virtue of our own. Intoxicated with unbroken success, we have become too self-sufficient to feel the necessity of redeeming and preserving grace, too proud to pray to the God that made us:

"It behooves us, then, to humble ourselves before the offended Power, to confess our national sins, and to pray for clemency and forgiveness." ("A Proclamation by the President of the United States of America," March 30, 1863, as cited in *Complete Works of Abraham Lincoln,* 1905, p. 236.)

Unless we as citizens of this nation forsake our sins, political and otherwise, and return to the fundamental principles of Christianity and of constitutional government, we will lose our political liberties, our free institutions, and will stand in jeopardy before God of losing our exaltation. I am in full agreement with the statement made by President J. Reuben Clark, Jr.: "I say to you that the price of liberty is and always has been, blood, human blood, and if our liberties are lost, we shall never regain them except at the price of blood. They must not be lost!" (*Stand Fast by Our Constitution,* p. 137.)

Yes, I repeat, righteousness is an indispensable ingredient to liberty. Virtuous people elect wise and good representatives. Good representatives make good laws and then wisely administer them. This tends to preserve righteousness. An unvirtuous citizenry tends to elect representatives who will pander to their covetous lustings. The burden of self-government is a great responsibility. It calls for restraint, righteousness, responsibility, and reliance upon God. It is a truism from the Lord that "when the wicked rule the people mourn." (D&C 98:9.)

As presiding officer of the constitutional convention, George Washington appealed to the delegates in these words: "Let us raise a standard to which the wise and the honest can repair." Wise and honorable men raised that glorious standard for this nation. It will also take wise and honorable men to perpetuate what was so nobly established.

A citizen of this republic cannot do his duty and be an idle spectator. How appropriate and vital it is today to remember this counsel from the Lord: "Honest men and wise men should be sought for diligently, and good men and wise men ye should observe to uphold." (D&C 98:10.)

Goodness, wisdom, and honesty are the three qualities of statesmanship, qualities this country needs more than ever before. May we be wise—prayerfully wise—in electing those who would lead us. May we select only those who understand and will adhere to constitutional principles. To do so, we need to understand these principles ourselves.

In 1973 the First Presidency of the Church made public this statement: "We urge members of the Church and all Americans to begin now to reflect more intently on the meaning and importance of the Constitution, and of adherence to its principles." (*Ensign,* November 1973, p. 90.)

May I urge every Latter-day Saint and all Americans in North and South America to become familiar with every part of this document. Many of the constitutions of countries in South America have been patterned in large measure after that of the United States. We should understand the Constitution as the founders meant that it should be understood. We can do this by reading their words about it, such as those contained in the Federalist Papers. Such understanding is essential if we are to preserve what God has given us.

I reverence the Constitution of the United States as a sacred document. To me its words are akin to the revelations of God, for God has placed His stamp of approval on the Constitution. I testify that the God of heaven selected and sent some of His choicest spirits to lay the foundation of this government as a prologue to the restoration of the gospel and the second coming of our Savior.

May God bless us to protect this sacred instrument. In the words of the Prophet Joseph Smith, "May those principles, which were so honorably and nobly defended, namely, the Constitution of our land, by our fathers, be established forever." (D&C 109:54.)

V

Our Priceless Pioneer Legacy

"We stand today as beneficiaries of the pioneers' priceless legacy to us—a legacy based on the solid truth that character is the one thing we develop in this world that we take with us into the next."

The historian Lord Macauly said, "The people who do not revere the deeds of their ancestors will never do anything to be remembered by their descendants."

We hope that the present generation will continue to be reminded by sermon, song, eulogy, and family traditions of the noble virtues of their pioneer ancestors and to recognize that it was by and through the hand of God that they were delivered from their oppressors and that the settlement in Ephraim's mountains took place.

Though others have said more eloquently what my tongue or pen could express, I deeply desire to pay reverent tribute to these heroes of the past, to their faithful deeds, their noble lives, and their lasting lessons of courage, faith, self-reliance, stamina, industry, and integrity. All generations have need of these virtues.

We stand today as beneficiaries of their priceless legacy to us, a legacy based on the solid truth that character is the one thing we develop in this world that we take with us into the next.

And what is that legacy?

The pioneers came to the Salt Lake Valley with credentials that spanned the centuries, a bloodline coursing through their veins from illustrious parentage: Abraham and Sarah; Isaac and Rebekah; Jacob and Rachel. Theirs was a bloodline preserved through four centuries of Egyptian captivity; an exile and exodus from the land of their captivity that lasted forty years—a time necessary for a new, less-enslaved generation to develop; and then a settlement in a promised land, which lasted over seven centuries. Theirs was a bloodline that endured a long dispersion and centuries of migrations that brought their sifted lineage into northern Europe and Great Britain.

When the tyranny of European governments disallowed freedom of religious worship, God prepared a new land of promise—the United States of America—where such freedom was eventually guaranteed by an inspired Constitution. Some of the progenitors of the pioneers came before the gospel's restoration, such as the ancestors of Joseph Smith, but most came following the restoration. They came with a self-identity that led President Brigham Young to exclaim on one occasion, "You understand who we are; we are of the House of Israel, of the royal seed, of the royal blood." (*Journal of Discourses* 2:269.)

They came with the faith that God had "set his hand a second time" to restore the house of Israel; that to accomplish His purposes and design, the Church of Jesus Christ had been restored again on the earth through the instrumentality of a latter-day prophet, Joseph Smith, Jr.; and that following the martyrdom, the keys of the priesthood had been continued through Joseph's ordained successor, Brigham Young. They believed themselves to be God-directed and prophet-led. That was the conviction which inspired their sacrifices.

They came with indomitable courage, following incredible suffering and adversity. Who can forget those almost insufferable conditions during their exodus? While they were encamped at Sugar Creek, Iowa, in February 1846, a raging blizzard left twelve inches of snow on the ground. Following that storm, the temperatures fell to twelve degrees below zero. On one of those cold nights nine babies were born. Eliza R. Snow provides this vivid account:

> Mothers gave birth to offspring under almost every variety of circumstances imaginable, except those to which they had been accustomed; some in tents, others in wagons—in rainstorms and in snowstorms. I heard of one birth which occurred under the rude shelter of a hut, the sides of which were formed of blankets fastened to poles stuck in the ground, with a bark roof through which the rain was dripping. Kind sisters stood holding dishes to catch the water as it fell, thus protecting the newcomer and its mother from a shower-bath as the little innocent first entered on the stage of human life; and through faith in the great ruler of events, no harm resulted to either.
>
> Let it be remembered that the mothers of these wilderness-born babies were not savages, accustomed to roam the forest and brave the storm and tempest—those who had never known the comforts and delicacies of civilization and refinement. They were not those who, in the wilds of nature, nursed their offspring amid reeds and rushes, or in the recesses of rocky caverns; most of them were born and educated in the Eastern States—and there embraced the Gospel as taught by Jesus and his Apostles; and, for the sake of their religion, had gathered with the Saints, and under trying circumstances had assisted, by their faith, patience and energies, in making Nauvoo what its name indicates "the beautiful." There they had lovely homes, decorated with flowers and enriched with choice fruit trees, just beginning to yield plentifully. (Edward W. Tullidge, *The Women of Mormondom*, pp. 307-9.)

In March of that same year, four hundred wagons set out toward the Rocky Mountains, but now a spring thaw had turned the ruts into a quagmire of mud.

> Under these testing conditions Orson Spencer's wife, a young woman of thirty-five, succumbed to this inclement life, leaving six children under fifteen years of age. Shortly before her passing, she opened her eyes and, seeing her children huddling by her bed, burst into tears, sobbing: "Oh, you dear little children! How I hope you will fall into kind hands when I am gone."
>
> Not a murmur escaped her lips. . . . The storm was severe, and the wagon covers leaked. Friends held milk pans over her bed to keep her dry. Her daughter states that shortly before her mother departed this life, that she rallied and whispered to her husband: "A heavenly messenger appeared to me tonight and told me that I had done and suffered enough, and that he had now come to convey me to a mansion of gold."
>
> After kissing each child in turn, she whispered to her husband: "I love you more than ever!—But you must let me go!" It was enough. Orson Spencer sorrowfully dedicated her to her Father in heaven, and a moment later she was gone to her crown of glory. (Carter Grant, *The Kingdom of God Restored,* Deseret Book Co., 1955, pp. 344-45.)

But all was not sorrow. "We outlived the trying scenes," wrote John Taylor. "We felt contented and happy—the songs of Zion resounded from wagon to wagon—from tent to tent." (*Millennial Star* 8:7.) It was under these conditions that William Clayton penned the verses to "All Is Well," a poem that became an anthem of faith for the Latter-day Saints.

> "We'll find the place which God for us prepared,
> Far away in the West,
> Where none shall come to hurt or make afraid;
> There the Saints will be blessed.
> We'll make the air with music ring,
> Shout praises to our God and King;
> Above the rest these words we'll tell—
> All is well! all is well!"
>
> —*Hymns,* no. 13

Little did Brother Clayton realize that his hymn would be sung by the 400-voice Tabernacle Choir before the president of the United States and other dignitaries at the commemoration of our nation's two hundredth birthday.

The pioneers came west with a devotion, patriotism, and loyalty to the nation that had silently sanctioned their expulsion from their homes and the loss of their possessions. History records no modern parallel to their epic exodus from Nauvoo, so it is little wonder that the situation of these modern Israelites was likened to their ancient ancestors exiled from Egypt. In fact, President Joseph F. Smith said that the pioneer feat of modern Israel exceeded that of their progenitors:

"A wonderful event has occurred in these last days among this people, an event many times more wonderful than the marching of the children of Israel from Egypt to the holy land. It is only a short distance from the River Jordan to the land of Egypt—only a few hundred miles—and yet they wandered about for forty years seeking the goodly land. . . . What has happened in this dispensation? This people have crossed deserts that are beyond comparison with those traversed by the children of Israel. They were not fed by manna it is true, although they were fed with quails in great abundance on at least one occasion, and they performed a journey nearly four times as great as that performed by the children of Israel—which occupied them forty years—in the course of a few months. . . .

"We were led out of bondage by the power of God. The angels of God and the power and presence of the Almighty accompanied us, so much so that notwithstanding the country was covered with sagebrush and crickets, presenting the most forbidding appearance President Young was enabled to point out where the Temple and city would be built. He said, 'You may go north and south, east and west, and explore the country all over, but when you have done it, you will come back and say that this is the spot where we are to settle.' " (*Journal of Discourses* 24:155-56.)

It is ironic that in the course of their exodus, this same government that stood by while they were forcibly expelled from Illinois should now come to them with a request for five hundred able-bodied men to fight in the war with Mexico. So disproportionate, inequitable, and unjust in terms of their numbers and their situation was the request for manpower that President Brigham Young commented later:

"Look . . . at the proportion of the number required of us, compared with that of any other portion of the Republic. A requisition of only thirty thousand from a population of more than twenty millions was all that was wanted, amounting to only one person and a half to a thousand inhabitants. If all other circumstances had been equal, . . . our quota of an equitable requisition would not have exceeded four persons. Instead of this, five hundred must go, thirteen thousand percent above an equal ration." (*Journal of Discourses* 2:174.)

But they did comply with the request—an extraordinary example of loyalty to their nation.

And what prompted such loyalty and patriotism? Not fear of reprisal, not servile obedience to their overlords, but a recognition that compliance with this request was the "interposition of that all-wise Being" who was bringing about their deliverance. "Thus," said Brigham Young, "were we saved from our enemies by complying with their . . . unjust and unparalleled exactions; again proving our loyalty to the Government." (Ibid.)

During the times of mobbings and persecutions, the revelations of God had prescribed the course of action they should take: importune for redress—at the feet of judges, at the feet of the governor, and at the feet of even the president of the United States. These steps were followed without relief, reparation, or redress. Under these conditions, I'm sure they questioned as did Joseph in Liberty Jail: "O God, where art thou? And where is the pavilion that covereth thy hiding place? How long shall thy hand be stayed? . . . O Lord, how long shall [thy people] suffer these wrongs and unlawful oppressions?" (D&C 121:1-3.)

They, who had suffered so much from oppressors, were to see that God takes His own retribution in His own time and in His own way; for as Lincoln said, "Nations, like individuals, are subjected to punishment and . . . may we not justly fear that the awful calamity of civil war which now desolates the land may be but a punishment inflicted upon us for our presumptuous sins. . . ." (A Proclamation by the President of the United States, March 30, 1863.)

While the Saints dwelt securely outside the boundaries of the United States, the nation was engaged in its most costly war in terms of lives lost, a civil war. No doubt these words of the Lord were recalled: "If the President heed [thee] not, then will the Lord arise and come forth out of his hiding place, and in his fury vex the nation." (D&C 101:89.)

It is a matter of history how truly those words were fulfilled.

Their loyalty to the nation extended not only from patriotism. It came also from a conviction that God had reserved this land for His purpose. It was a choice land above all others. The Constitution of this country had been established "by the hands of wise men whom [God] raised up unto this very purpose," and they were under divine commandment to maintain that inspired document "for the rights and protection of all flesh, according to just and holy principles." (D&C 101:80, 77.) And so, when they settled in this western haven, they fashioned a civil government in accord with the Constitution, which, in the hands of good and honorable men, would afford them and others their rights and liberty.

They came, with faith and industry, and carved an Eden out of a desert. Their promised land has become a prosperous valley. Commodious brick homes and apartment dwellings have replaced the log cabins. Luxuriant greenery, gardens, trees, and flowers flourish where once sagebrush and parched soil thrived. A tabernacle and magnificent temple have replaced the Bowery and Endowment House. Elaborate meetinghouses of worship fill the valley. Schools, seminaries, institutes, colleges, trade schools, and a university provide for secular and spiritual education. Stores, banks, factories abound. Truly, we live in the lap of luxury amid an unbounded prosperity, and all this because of the philosophy of self-reliance, initiative, personal industry, and faith in God.

Our forefathers gloried in hard work, but at the same time they drew liberally upon their prodigious spiritual reserves. They did not place their trust "in the arm of flesh." They were strong and courageous in the Lord, knowing that He was their defense, their refuge, their salvation. Strengthened by this faith, they relied on their cherished independence, their frugality, and honest toil. And history records that even the climate was tempered for their sakes, and their humble untiring efforts made "the desert to blossom as the rose."

Their faith was renewed by two of Isaiah's remarkable prophecies concerning the last days—the days in which they knew they were living. In the first of these Isaiah announces: "The wilderness and the solitary place shall be glad for them; and the desert shall rejoice, and blossom as the rose." (Isaiah 35:1.) And again: "For the Lord shall comfort Zion: he will comfort all her waste places; and he will make her wilderness like Eden, and her desert like the garden of the Lord; joy and gladness shall be found therein, thanksgiving, and the voice of melody." (Isaiah 51:3.)

And while their natural eyes saw only their log cabins and immediate surroundings, they envisioned the day when the words of Micah would be fulfilled: "But in the last days it shall come to pass, that the mountain of the house of the Lord shall be established in the top of the mountains, and it shall be exalted above the hills; and people shall flow unto it. And many nations shall come, and say, Come, and let us go up to the mountain of the Lord, and to the house of the God of Jacob; and he will teach us his ways, and we will walk in his paths: for the law shall go forth of Zion, and the word of the Lord from Jerusalem." (Micah 4:1-2.)

We have witnessed the fulfillment of these remarkable prophecies. But today, a contrary philosophy has come into the land. It is one that espouses that government benefits should replace the fruits of individual initiative and labor.

Such a philosophy can result only in the shackling of man's liberties—in the eventual destruction of our freedom. Had the early settlers throughout the land lived by such a philosophy, this glorious nation of ours would be a vast untamed wilderness known only to the Indians who had lived here for centuries before. I earnestly pray that this important lesson of history shall not go unheeded.

Yes, they came to the valleys of the mountains—first a trickle, the advance party on July 21 and 22, and then, on the 24th, the main caravan of 143 men, three women, and two children. The trickle of immigrants was followed by the hundreds, then the thousands, so that by 1869 more than 68,000 Mormon pioneers had crossed the plains. They came with their faith, loyalty, courage, industry, and integrity. Their legacy to us may be summarized in these fitting words by the late President J. Reuben Clark, Jr.:

"God has never worked out his purposes through the pampered victims of ease and luxury and riotous living. Always he has used to meet the great crises in his work, those in whom hardship, privation, and persecution had built characters and wills of iron. God shapes his servants in the forge of adversity; he does not fashion them in the hothouse of ease and luxury." (Address delivered at dedication of "This Is the Place" monument, July 24, 1947; in *Improvement Era* 50:573.)

However outmoded some of these standards may be considered today, they are nonetheless enduring truths without which no character worthy of the name can be built. We have respectfully called them pioneers, because they prepared the way for us to follow. May we possess courage to direct our lives in accordance with the enduring values so represented by their lives.

VI

Can We Preserve What They Wrought?

"Were the Founding Fathers and pioneer forefathers to counsel us today in their fundamental beliefs, so manifest by their acts, what would they say to us?"

Today we live in a land choice above all other lands. We live amid unbounded prosperity—this because of the heritage bequeathed to us by our forebears—a heritage of self-reliance, initiative, personal industry, and faith in God, all in an atmosphere of freedom.

Were these Founding Fathers and pioneer forefathers to counsel us today in their fundamental beliefs, so manifest by their acts, what would they say to us?

First: They would counsel us to have faith in God. It was by this faith that they were sustained in their privations, sacrifices, and suffering. They placed their trust in God. He was their defense, their refuge, and their salvation. Their faith is perhaps best expressed by the father of our country, George Washington: "The success, which has hitherto attended our united efforts, we owe to the gracious interposition of Heaven; and to that interposition let us gratefully ascribe the praise of victory, and the blessings of peace." (To the Executive of New Hampshire, November 3, 1789, *Writings,* 12:175.)

Yes, it was this faith in God that sustained them in their hours of extremity. We too will need this same faith to sustain us in the critical days ahead.

Second: They would counsel us to strengthen our homes and family ties. Though they did not possess our physical comforts, they left their posterity a legacy of something more enduring: a hearthside where parents were close by their children, where daily devotions, family prayer, scripture reading, and the singing of hymns were commonplace. Families worked, worshiped, played, and prayed together. Family home evening, now a once-a-week practice among the Saints, was to our pioneer forebears almost a nightly occurrence.

Can we not see in their examples the solutions to problems threatening families today? Were we to pattern our homes accordingly, divorce would be eliminated, children would be welcomed and guided, and love between parents and children would abound. There would be no generation gap. Family unity and solidarity, crowned with love and happiness, would prevail.

Third: They would counsel us in the dignity of work, to practice thrift, and to be self-sustaining. Theirs was a philosophy that neither the world nor government owes a man his bread. Man is commanded by God to live by the sweat of his own brow, not someone else's. In his First Inaugural Address, Thomas Jefferson counseled us toward a wise and frugal government, one that "shall not take from the mouth of labor the bread it had earned."

The Founding Fathers would be in complete agreement with this counsel from Brigham Young: "Beautify your gardens, your houses, your farms; beautify the city. This will make us happy, and produce plenty." (*Discourses of Brigham Young,* p. 302.) "To be slothful, wasteful, lazy and indolent . . . is unrighteous." (*Ibid.,* p. 303.) "Learn to sustain yourselves; lay up grain and flour, and save it against a day of scarcity." (*Ibid.,* p. 293.) ". . . If you cannot obtain all you wish for today, learn to do without." (*Ibid.,* p. 293.) "Be prompt in everything, and especially to pay your debts." (*Ibid.,* p. 303.)

Finally: These noble founders and pioneers—our benefactors—would counsel us to preserve the freedoms granted to us by God. They knew that the foundation of this nation was spiritual, that the source of all our blessings was God. They knew that this nation can only prosper in an atmosphere of freedom.

Those intrepid forebears knew that their righteousness was the indispensable ingredient to liberty, that this was the greatest legacy they could pass on to future generations. They would counsel us to preserve this liberty by alert righteousness. Righteousness is always measured by a nation or an individual keeping the commandments of God.

In the outer office of the Council of Twelve hangs a painting by Utah artist Arnold Friberg, depicting George Washington, the father of our country, on his knees at Valley Forge. That painting symbolizes the faith of our forebears. I wish it could be in every American home.

In the 1940s, while serving as the executive officer of the National Council of Farmer Cooperatives in Washington, D.C., I saw in a Hilton Hotel a placard depicting Uncle Sam, representing America, on his knees in humility and prayer. Beneath the placard was the inscription "Not beaten there by the hammer and sickle, but freely, responsibly, confidently. . . . We need fear nothing or no one save God."

That picture has stayed in my memory ever since. America on her knees—in recognition that all our blessings come from God! America on her knees—out of a desire to serve the God of this land by keeping His commandments! America on her knees—not driven there in capitulation to some despotic government, but on her knees freely, willingly, gratefully! This is the sovereign remedy to all of our problems and the preservation of our liberties.

Yes, those valiant patriots and pioneers left us a great heritage. Are we prepared to do what they did? Will we pledge our lives, our possessions, our sacred honor for future generations and the upbuilding of God's kingdom on this earth?

Hear the challenge made to us—their descendants and benefactors—at the dedication of "This Is the Place" monument, at the mouth of Emigration Canyon, July 24, 1947:

"Can we keep and preserve what they wrought? Shall we pass on to our children the heritage they left us, or shall we lightly fritter it away? Have we their faith, their bravery, their courage; could we endure their hardships and suffering, make their sacrifices, bear up under their trials, their sorrow, their tragedies, believe the simple things they knew were true, have the simple faith that worked miracles for them, follow, and not falter or fall by the wayside, where our leaders advance, face the slander and the scorn of an unpopular belief? Can we do the thousands of little and big things that made them the heroic builders of a great Church, a great commonwealth?" (J. Reuben Clark, Jr., Address at the Dedication of "This Is the Place" Monument, July 24, 1947; in *Improvement Era* 50:626.)

There should be no doubt what our task is today. If we truly cherish the heritage we have received, we must maintain the same virtues and the same character of our stalwart forebears—faith in God, courage, industry, frugality, self-reliance, and integrity. We have the obligation to maintain what those who pledged their lives, their fortunes, and their sacred honor gave to future generations. Our opportunity and obligation for doing so is clearly upon us. May we begin to repay this debt by preserving and strengthening this heritage in our own lives, in the lives of our children, their children, and generations yet unborn.

Our Present Challenge

*"Our problems today
are essentially problems of the spirit. . . .
The solution is personal
and national reformation.
In short, it is to bring our national character
ahead of our technological
and material advances.
Repentance is the sovereign remedy
to our problems."*

VII

Problems Affecting
Our Domestic Tranquillity

"We are rearing a generation that does not seem to understand the fundamentals of our American way of life, a generation that is no longer dedicated to its preservation. . . . We can only appreciate freedom if we understand the comparative fruits thereof."

One of the problems that always confronts a physician while examining a patient who complains of a malady is to distinguish between the disease and its symptoms. To treat only symptoms without effecting a cure will cause the disease to run its fatal course.

In our country, we know there are disorders and malfunctionings of various kinds in our body politic and our economic and social order because of the general symptoms; to name but a few, rampant inflation, increased crime, sexual permissiveness, more incidence of broken homes, excessive national and consumer debt, discontent among labor, women, and minorities, and disillusionment among our youth. With all the palliatives being advanced as cure-alls, it seems significant to ask: Are the remedies we are applying directed to conquering the actual disease, or are they merely palliatives to relieve the inconvenience and distress of the symptoms, while the disease, cancer-like, takes us to our destruction?

Before we go to our ailments and disorders, it is well to review the elements of our health and strength that we have acquired under our divinely inspired Constitution, the liberties it guarantees, and the free institution it sets up.

The facts speak for themselves: No nation on earth eats as well as our nation. No country is so well clothed. No people are so well housed. No individuals on this earth have so many of the conveniences as we do in terms of heating, lighting, plumbing, and other comforts. These are not luxuries enjoyed by the rich alone; these are the comforts of us, the common people—comforts of which mighty monarchs of bygone ages never dreamed.

No nation has such an industrial complex made available to it because of applied science and the harnessing, in part, of electricity. Our transportation system hardly knows any bounds on this sphere. We travel in our planes, trains, cars, and buses without limitation in our country, and in relative luxury, a luxury scarcely affordable or even accessible to masses of humanity in other countries.

No other country has such an elaborate and universally accessible educational system where even the humblest among us can climb the ladder of success to the highest rung. The "Horatio Alger" story is yet going on every day in this country.

Few nations enjoy such freedoms—freedom to speak, freedom to own property and business or participate in ownership, freedom to worship, freedom to print, freedom to travel at home and abroad, freedom to censure even public officials, and freedom to have the privacy we desire.

No country has been more concerned with due process in its judicial system than ours. The protection of human rights, as granted by our Constitution and Bill of Rights, is not just theory. History will record that we bent over backwards to protect the rights of the individual, sometimes even to a fault.

No other country has been so generous as America in terms of its money and food. No other nation has fought starvation and economic collapse and come to the rescue of nations struck by natural disaster as America has.

There are many more blessings, but these are a few we might enumerate. Whence came these blessings? To those who would malign our country or system, we ask, by what source did we receive such prosperity?

The power has come to us from God, because, to a great extent, we have been a God-fearing, Christ-worshiping people. There are some in this land who believe this is "a land choice above all other lands" to the Lord, and that we shall remain here on this land as we remain in God's divine favor.

There are principles which, if applied and acted upon, are conducive to the social, spiritual, and economic well-being of the nation. They are basic to sound international as well as domestic accord. They came from God himself to Moses, and form the foundation for civilized society. They are embodied in what has been denominated as the Ten Commandments. These were designed by an Omniscient Intelligence to plumb the depths of human motives and urges and to govern the baser parts of man's nature. It is well to be reminded that no nation has ever perished that has kept the commandments of God.

The commandments, known as the Decalogue, stipulate first the sovereignty of God, providing for our allegiance to Him. This is followed by the declaration of treason against Him with its attendant punishment, even to the proclamation of the great law of heredity operative upon transgressors. Then follows the law against blasphemy, declaring that those who blaspheme will not be held guiltless. These constitute the first three commandments and circumscribe man's relationships with God.

The balance of the Decalogue deals with man's relationships with his fellowman. There is the promulgation of law governing family relationships, parent and child; the law that specifies periods of work and rest, the relationship of capital and labor; the principles that govern civic relationships and declare social order—the "thou shalt nots." The relationship of these commandments to the domestic problems in our society today may well be in order.

Let us take the first—the worship of and service to God. Worship and belief in God have been basic to our social, economic, and political life during the medieval and modern eras. They have been the anchor to which we were moored, the foundation of our Judaic-Christian culture. But today that worship, that belief, is waning. We are so puffed up with our material achievements that we doubt all that we cannot see, smell, taste, feel, or hear, or that we cannot bring under our will. We think thus, notwithstanding the limitation of our knowledge and the fact that we are constantly finding more and more to learn of the hitherto unknown. Yet we hesitate on the one great ultimate fact, that we had a Creator, God. As Lincoln declared during the Civil War, so now may we say, "We have forgotten God."

"Thou shalt not take the name of the Lord thy God in vain; for the Lord will not hold him guiltless that taketh his name in vain." (Exodus 20:7.) The stage, the screen, the novel, the club conversation, the street discussion, too often the fireside intimacies are punctuated with blasphemy, to which may be added, as of the same nature, coarse, ribald jokes, foul stories, and low small-talk. God's law forbids blasphemy. To break it brings its own punishment.

Next is the keeping of the Sabbath. Many—too many—have almost ceased to observe the Sabbath. Not only is it a workday now, but it is supremely a day of amusement and recreation: golf, skiing, skating, hunting, fishing, picnicking, racing, movies, theaters, ball playing, dancing, and other forms of fun-making, all are coming largely to be the rule among too many so-called Christians. Some churches are said to encourage all these, if properly conducted. But God's law says, keep the Sabbath day holy. "Six days shalt thou labour, and do all thy work." (Exodus 20:9.) We are becoming an idle people. More and more we expect to live with little or no work. Hours of work become shorter and shorter; pay, therefore, becomes greater and greater. But finally we shall reach the minimum of work. It takes so many man-hours to raise the necessary foods to sustain a man's life and to provide the other necessities of clothing, shelter, and fuel. In the last analysis, this will measure the minimum working day and its compensation. Machinery will reduce the time somewhat as compared with hand labor, but skilled labor costs more, and so the lessened time tends to waste the increased efficiency, and we are somewhere near where we were. It always has, over the long pull, taken six full days in each week, barring vacations (and these cannot be too long, nor too frequent), to produce a livelihood.

Next comes "Honour thy father and thy mother" (Exodus 20:12), which Christ declared meant to support them. Yet never before in recorded history has this law of God been so violated as it is today. Untold thousands of children in this nation have abandoned their parents to the care of the state. This action has brought in its wake a host of other ills: idleness, greed, covetousness, cheating, hiding property, lying about it, and the adoption by the child and parent of any device that could bring the parent within the provisions of the dole law. The violation of this law of God in our day has carried such a speedy visitation of many of its penalties that even the blind might see and the deaf hear and the witless understand, if they wish.

"Thou shalt not kill." (Exodus 20:13.) We still frown on murder, but need we be reminded in what small esteem life is now held? Men are to live, else they could not work out their destiny. This mandate was given to Israel and to each child thereof. It is the command not to commit the sin of Cain. It is binding upon every one of God's children. It speaks to them as individuals; it commands them as associated together in nations. It covers the single case of another Abel; it embraces the mass slaughter of war. It is the law higher than the law of punishment: "Eye for eye, tooth for tooth, hand for hand, foot for foot." (Exodus 21:24.) It forecast the Master's law of love and forgiveness: "Love your enemies, bless them that curse you, do good to them that hate you, and pray for them which despitefully use you, and persecute you." (Matthew 5:44.)

"Thou shalt not commit adultery," and also, "Thou shalt not covet thy neighbour's wife." (Exodus 20:14, 17.) Here God gives the great law of chastity that lies at the base of purity of family blood and the undefiled home. When the ancient prophets desired to excoriate Israel for her sins, they did it by comparing her to the prostitute. In the category of sins, unchastity stands next to murder, nor may we forget that growing crime of abortion, which usually follows unchastity. Never in this generation of ours have morals been so loose as now. Sex is all but deified, and yet at the same time, it is put before youth in its lowest, coarsest, and most debasing forms. The curtain of modesty has been torn aside, and in play, book, and movie and television, in magazine story, picture, and advertisement, immorality stands out in all its vulgarity and rottenness.

"Thou shalt not steal." (Exodus 20:15.) What do our criminal court records disclose on this—records that are filled with accounts of juvenile delinquencies in numbers never before equaled in this country? When God commanded "Thou shalt not steal," He thereby recognized the fundamental right of property. How slight today is the popular regard for the property of others that, seen and desired, is too often forcibly appropriated.

"Thou shalt not bear false witness." (Exodus 20:16.) The violations of God's laws tell us that false witnessing, lying, is not absent from us. Yet God's law is a law of truthfulness.

Then comes "Thou shalt not covet." (Exodus 20:17.) Covetousness is one of the besetting sins of this generation, and our covetousness reaches every item forbidden in the commandments—our neighbor's house, his wife, his help, his worldly goods, and everything that is our neighbor's. Covetousness, plus love of idleness, lies at the root of our violation of the law of work, with all the ills that has brought. Covetousness has invaded our homes, our communities, the nations of the world. It has brought with it greed, avarice, ambition, and love of power. Men scheme, plan, overreach, cheat, and lie to get their neighbor's heritage. Covetousness threatens the peace of the world today more than any other one element. But God said, "Thou shalt not covet."

Two other commandments we must note. On the Sabbath, when Jesus came riding into Jerusalem upon an ass, the Sadducees, scribes, and Pharisees came to Him in the temple, vainly trying to entrap Him, that they might arrest and wreak their vengeance upon Him. One of the Pharisees, a lawyer, asked of Him: "Which is the great commandment in the law?" And Jesus, quoting the law given to Israel under Moses from Leviticus, replied: "Thou shalt love the Lord thy God with all thy heart, and with all thy soul, and with all thy mind. This is the first and great commandment. And the second is like unto it. Thou shalt love thy neighbour as thyself. On these two commandments hang all the law and the prophets." (Matthew 22:35-40.) These Mosaic laws contain the basic principles upon which all civilized governments and our present civilization have been built. As man is now constituted, neither permanent government nor civilization can be built in violation of these principles. A little reflection will persuade any right-thinking person of this.

It must be remembered that the Founding Fathers of this great nation were men imbued by these principles. There are those in the land whose faith it is that these were "wise men whom [God] raised up" for the purpose of establishing the Constitution of the United States. They recognized that there are two possible sources to the origin of our freedoms we have come to know as human rights. Rights are either God-given as part of a divine plan or they are granted as part of the political plan. Reason, necessity, and religious conviction and belief in the sovereignty of God led these men to accept the *divine* origin of these rights. To God's glory and the credit of these men, our nation was uniquely born.

If we accept the premise that human rights are granted by government, then we must be willing to accept the corollary that they can be denied by government. If Americans should ever come to believe that their rights and freedoms are instituted among men by politicians and bureaucrats, then they will no longer carry the proud inheritance of their forefathers, but will grovel before their masters seeking favors and dispensations—a throwback to the feudal system of the Dark Ages. We need to keep before us the truth that people who do not master themselves and their appetites will soon be mastered by government.

We are rearing a generation that does not seem to understand the fundamentals of our American way of life, a generation that is no longer dedicated to its preservation. Our people, both before and after they arrive at the age of the right of the ballot, should understand what it is that has made America great. We can only appreciate freedom if we understand the comparative fruits thereof. It was Jefferson who said, "The price of freedom is eternal vigilance." It is one thing to win freedom; its preservation is equally important. If reference is made continually to weaknesses of the private enterprise system without any effort to point out its virtues and the comparative fruits of this and other systems, the tendency in this country will be to demand that the government take over more and more of the economic and social responsibilities and make more of the decisions for the people. This can result in but one thing: slavery of the individual to the state. This seems to be the trend in the world today. The issue is whether the individual exists for the state or the state for the individual.

In a republic the real danger is that we may slowly slide into a condition of slavery of the individual to the state rather than entering this condition by a sudden revolution. The loss of our liberties might easily come about, not through the ballot box, but through the death of incentive to work, to earn, and to save. Such a condition is usually brought about by a series of little steps which, at the time, seem justified by a variety of reasons, and which may on the surface appear to be laudable as to intent. It has been pointed out that the more basic reasons offered by would-be planned economy advocates are "the desire to change and control others, the search for security, and the desire of individuals or groups to improve their own economic status or that of others by means of direct governmental intervention."

It also seems fundamental to ask, Are we rearing a generation of Americans who do not understand the basis of our economic prosperity and the principles upon which prosperity is predicated?

In 1801 Thomas Jefferson, in his First Inaugural Address, said: ". . . with all these blessings, what more is necessary to make us a happy and prosperous people? Still one thing more, fellow citizens—a wise and frugal government, which shall restrain men from injuring one another, which shall leave them otherwise free to regulate their own pursuits or industry and improvement, and shall not take from the mouth of labor the bread it has earned." (Saul K. Padover, *The Complete Jefferson,* New York: Tudor Publishing Company, 1943, p. 386.)

America was built on a certain pattern of industry. It was one that was discovered by the Plymouth Colony after trying an experiment with socialism, which brought the colony to the brink of famine. Governor Bradford, with the approval of the chief men of the colony, set aside the social experiment whereby the most able and fit expended their strength and industry to support other men's wives and children—"a kind of slaverie" that they deemed repugnant. He then "assigned to every family a parcell of land according to the proportion of their number for that end." "This," he said, "had very good success; for it made all hands very industrious, so as much more corne was planted than other waise would have bene. . . . The women now wente willingly into the field, and tooke their little ones with them to set corne, which before would aledg weakness, and inabilitie; whom to have compelled would have bene thought great tiranie and oppression." (William T. David, ed., *Bradford's History of Plantation, 1606-1646,* 1908, pp. 146f.)

The principles behind this American philosophy can be reduced to a rather simple formula:

1. Economic security for all is impossible without abundance.

2. Abundance is impossible without industrious and efficient production.

3. Such production is impossible without energetic, willing, and eager labor.

4. This is not possible without incentive.

5. Of all forms of incentive, the freedom to attain a reward for one's labor is the most sustaining for most people. Sometimes called the profit motive, it is simply the right to plan and to earn and to enjoy the fruits of your labor.

6. This profit motive diminishes as government controls, regulations, and taxes increase to deny the fruits of success to those who produce.

7. Therefore, any attempt through government intervention to redistribute the material rewards of labor can only result in the eventual destruction of the productive base of society, without which real abundance and security for more than the ruling elite are quite impossible.

It is evident that when the willingness to work sharply declines, there will be increased frustration of any economic plan, however well intentioned or well conceived. Poverty is abolished by economic growth, not by economic distribution, and economic growth requires work. As we become more and more welfare conscious, it is essential to reaffirm the scriptural imperative that the idler shall not eat the bread of the worker. (See Proverbs 31:27.) To operate contrary to this is soul-destroying to the idler and incentive-reducing to the worker.

Many of our problems and dangers center in the issues of so-called fair prices, wages, and profits and the relationship between management and labor. We must realize that it is just as possible for wages to be too high as it is for prices and profits to be excessive. There is a tendency, of course, for almost everyone to feel that his share is unfair, whether it is or not. An effort to adjust apparent inequities often calls for government subsidies. Too often these are authorized without asking, "Who will pay for them?" Much of our program of letting the government pay for it can be described as an attempt to better yourself by increasing your pay to yourself and then sending yourself the bill.

The only safe and solid answer is the mechanism of a free market operating in an enterprise and free competition. Here everyone has a chance to cast his vote in the election that will decide what is a fair price, fair wage, and fair profit, and what should be produced and in what quantities. To contradict the justice of that decision is to contradict the whole concept of justice by the democratic process. All will agree that the democratic process and the free market—both parts of our American way of life—are not perfect, but they are believed to have fewer faults and to do a better job than any other known device. A sure way to take a shortcut to serfdom is to discard the sovereign rights of all the people in either the political or the economic realm.

We must remember that government assistance and control are essentially political provisions, and that experience has demonstrated that, for that reason, they are not sufficiently stable to warrant their utilization as a foundation for sound economic growth under a free enterprise system. The best way—the American way—is still maximum freedom for the individual guaranteed by a wise government that establishes and enforces the rules of the game. Good government, which guarantees the maximum of freedom, liberty, and development to the individual, must be based upon sound principles; and we must ever remember that ideas and principles are either sound or unsound in spite of those who hold them. Freedom of achievement has achieved and will continue to produce the maximum of benefits in terms of human welfare.

Economic blessings are obtained by being obedient to the laws upon which economic blessings are predicated.

As we rightly concern ourselves over pressing domestic problems—problems that affect the tranquillity of our people—it is well to remember that just as physical laws are interrelated, so are spiritual laws. It is much less likely that someone will be concerned with his adverse impact on the environment and his neighbors if he does not love his neighbors. One dimension of spiritual law, therefore, is that one's self-regard and his esteem for his fellowmen are intertwined. If there is disregard for one's self, there is bound to be some disregard for one's neighbor. If there isn't reverence for life itself, there is apt to be little reverence for the resources God has placed here on which we must call. The outward expressions of irreverence for God, for life, and for our fellowmen take the form of things like littering, heedless strip mining, heedless pollution of water and air. But these are, after all, outward expressions of the inner man. Those who undertake the task of alerting their fellowmen with regard to physical ecology without also paying heed to spiritual laws have undertaken an impossible task. If we are not really the children of our Heavenly Father, who placed us here by design and for a purpose, and if there are not absolute spiritual as well as physical laws that we violate at our peril, then man has to be appealed to on different grounds, and that is a task that is next to impossible. For if we are merely transients in an unexplainable world, we will act more as tourists than residents!

The Lord has said: "Yea, all things which come of the earth, in the season thereof, are made for the benefit and the use of man, both to please the eye and to gladden the heart; Yea, for food and for raiment, for taste and for smell, to strengthen the body and to enliven the soul. And it pleaseth God that he hath given all these things unto man; for unto this end were they made to be used, with judgment, not to excess, neither by extortion." (D&C 59:18-20.)

The Lord has told us with regard to the essential resources of this planet that "there is enough and to spare." (D&C 104:17.) What is lacking so often is not the engineering to produce that grows out of the world of technology, but the human engineering necessary to share that which we have. Sharing with generations yet unborn, however, is also rooted in brotherhood and love.

Whatever mortal reasons there are to be concerned about environment, there are eternal reasons, too, for us to be thoughtful stewards. President Brigham Young said: "Not one particle of all that comprises this vast creation of God is our own. Everything we have has been bestowed upon us for our action, to see what we would do with it—whether we would use it for eternal life and exaltation, or for eternal death and degradation."

We are also rightfully concerned about the fabric of our country's home life. Another president of the Church, David O. McKay, soberly reminded us that "no other success in life can compensate for failure in the home." As society draws women out of the home unnecessarily, as we tax ourselves to then make up for failures in the home, we substitute some programs that are really self-defeating and counterproductive. We err spiritually in doing so. If we are really concerned about alienation, we must do everything we can to spare the family, since it is the basic source of love, discipline, and values. Love at home is one of the basic needs in life, a spiritual law which, if violated, brings harsh, irrevocable consequences. One writer has said, "For when we emit from our families unloved, undisciplined individuals into the stream of humanity, this is more dangerous than emitting raw sewage." It is clear that we cannot have peace in the world, for instance, without harmony in the home.

We are concerned about scarred landscapes that cause floods and leave an economic emptiness that haunts the coming generations. Similarly, unchastity leaves terrible scars, brings floods of tears and anguish, and leaves a moral emptiness. Significantly, both imprudent strip mining and unchastity rest on a life-style that partakes of an "eat, drink, and be merry" philosophy—gouge and grab now without regard to the consequences. Both negligent strip mining and unchastity violate the spirit of stewardship over our planet and person.

Some may ask why we as a people and church quietly and consistently seek to change individuals while there are such large problems all about us, such as the so-called urban crisis. But decaying cities are simply a delayed reflection of decaying individuals; revenue shortages are real, but the shortfall in character is one of its causes. The commandments of God give emphasis to improvement of the individual as the only real way to bring about real improvement in society. Until we focus on basic qualities, little progress will be made.

So much depends, therefore, on our basic desires and attitudes. Just as our political democracy depends greatly on our capacity for self-discipline, so our capacity for self-discipline depends, in turn, on our having fundamental values and reasons to check our appetites and our passions. Otherwise, our plunder of people more than matches our plunder of mountains.

It has been said that we cannot tame our technology until we can tame ourselves, and that we cannot tame our cities to make them good and habitable until we can tame ourselves. It is so, and always has been the case, that the outward things depend on the inward commitments.

This nation now struggles for balance between the need for energy and food production, on the one hand, and our need to extract these things wisely, on the other hand. If the proponents in the political process are unduly selfish, then the balance will not be struck, and there will be strife, suffering, and waste. When, however, we have esteem for each other—shared respect as well as shared concerns—then economic and political accommodations are possible, and wise balance is more probable.

While the resources of this planet are both perishable and renewable, time cannot be recycled. We are reminded in God's early communications with mankind that when our time, for instance, is given over too much for the seeking of pleasure, then the serious and eternal things are left undone. If we become pleasure-seekers, we will plunder our environment much more rapidly than if we have a sense of history—not only about this planet, but also about the people who live thereon.

We hear a great deal about the spiraling cost and incidence of juvenile delinquency and crime in our nation. Overcrowded living conditions are not a cause for crime, though they might contribute to it. We must look elsewhere: the failure of parents to teach their children to walk uprightly before the Lord; the failure of parents and communities to provide youth opportunities to work; and the failure of elected officials to develop a welfare program that is based on work and that will restore dignity to the individual.

We talk about cleaning up our water resources, our landscapes, national parks, and atmosphere. Suppose $120 billion were available to do this? Then we think of the horrendous cost of crime, the cost of alcoholism, the cost of smoking, the cost of gambling, and the cost of insurance and commodities to so many because of recklessness, irresponsibility, shoplifting, and dishonesty. The problem reduces down to an individual matter of man keeping the commandments of God and the laws of his society.

The Church of Jesus Christ of Latter-day Saints is making significant contributions to solutions on our domestic problems, including the following:

1. *We are urging our Church membership to stabilize the family unit.* We teach and emphasize that the key to family stability is a happy marriage based on family worship. Divorce is deplored. Indeed, at a general conference of the Church held in Salt Lake City, President Spencer W. Kimball said, "We decry divorce and feel that there are relatively few divorces which are justifiable. Great care should be taken in forming marriage alliances; then both parties should do their utmost to keep these marriages happy ones." (*Ensign,* November 1975, p. 6.)

We are actively engaged in teaching fathers to be compassionate fathers and mothers full-time mothers in the home. Fathers are commanded to take the lead in all spiritual matters. We encourage parents to teach their children fundamental spiritual principles that will instill faith in God, faith in their family, and faith in their country. These principles are embodied within an attractively prepared family home evening manual. Families are urged to hold a family night at least once a week. We have found that this program has met with great success.

2. *We teach and reteach to our Church membership the fundamental principles of work, thrift, dignity, and self-reliance so that the individual can eradicate from his life all tendencies toward idleness, unnecessary debt, and waste.* In 1936, during the midst of the depression, the Church established its well-known welfare plan. Its primary purpose was and is "to set up, in so far as it might be possible, a system under which the curse of idleness would be done away with, the evils of a dole abolished, and independence, industry, thrift and self respect be once more established amongst our people. The aim of the Church is to help the people to help themselves. Work is to be re-enthroned as the

ruling principle of the lives of our Church membership." (Heber J. Grant, *Conference Report,* October 1936, p. 3.)

The program is premised on the principle that all able-bodied men (the infirm and sick are in a different category) are entitled to have the opportunity to earn and acquire the necessities and the essential comforts of life, which embrace food, clothing, shelter, hospitalization, education, amusement and cultural activities, and, above all, opportunity for spiritual growth and joy. No true citizen, while physically able, will voluntarily shift from himself the burden of his own support. If the individual cannot support himself, he should look to his family for assistance. If the family cannot help, the Church may provide necessary sustenance—not as a dole, but in exchange for earned labor. It was never intended that man should live off the labors of someone else. Therein lies the key to sound economic management in the home as well as the nation.

3. *We urge our members to stay out of debt, to save what they can from their income, to store at least a year's supply of food, clothing, and other necessities, to pay a full tithing, and to support the poor and needy.* By following these principles, we believe, four immediate benefits accrue to the individual: (1) he will not be confronted with the danger of losing all he has should inflation or depression occur; (2) he will not be aiding in contributing to nationwide inflation; (3) he will have savings and supplies for emergencies; and (4) he may receive the blessings of God and his protecting care.

4. *We encourage all of our young people to acquire as much advanced training and education as will befit their chosen vocation so they will be well trained to make a contribution to their society.* It is well recognized that Utah, in terms of educational training, takes a back seat to no state in terms of per capita advanced education. Outsiders who have studied our system attribute this success to such fundamental teachings of the Church as "the glory of God is intelligence" (D&C 93:36), and "if a person gains more knowledge and intelligence in this life through his diligence and obedience than another, he will have so much the advantage in the world to come" (D&C 130:19). President Brigham Young insisted: "Learn everything that the children of men know, and be prepared for the most refined society upon the face of the earth, then improve on this until we are prepared and permitted to enter the society of the blessed—the holy angels that dwell in the presence of God. . . ." (*Discourses of Brigham Young,* p. 254.) We educate not only for time, but for eternity, and we demonstrate this by the fact that we willingly tax ourselves to support a Church educa-

tional system that provides religious training in connection with secular studies at the high school and college level.

5. *We urge our people to support the Constitution of the United States and our free institutions set up under it.* It is a part of our faith that the Constitution of the United States was inspired of God. We reverence it akin to the revelations that have come from God. The Church, out of respect for the rights of all its members to have their political views and loyalties, must maintain the strictest possible neutrality. We have no intention of trying to interfere with the fullest and freest exercise of the political franchise of our members under and within our Constitution, which the Lord declared He established "by the hands of wise men whom [He] raised up unto this very purpose" (D&C 101:80), and which, as to the principles thereof, the Prophet Joseph Smith, dedicating the Kirtland Temple, prayed should be "established forever" (D&C 109:54). The Church does not yield any of its devotion to our convictions about safeguarding the American principles and the establishment of government under federal and state constitutions and the civil rights of men safeguarded by these.

We warn our people about false political "isms" that have crept into our midst, revolutionists who use the technique that is as old as the human race—a fervid but false solicitude for the unfortunate over whom they thus gain mastery and control. We have consistently warned our people against the insidious nature of communism, which debases the individual, robs him of his agency, and makes him an enslaved tool of the state to which he must look for sustenance and religion. Latter-day Saints cannot be true to their faith and lend aid, encouragement, or sympathy to false idealogies such as socialism and communism. The official Church position on communism remains unchanged since it was first promulgated in 1936: "We call upon all Church members completely to eschew Communism. The safety of our divinely inspired Constitutional government and the welfare of our Church imperatively demand that Communism shall have no place in America." (*Improvement Era,* August 1936, p. 488.)

Let history bear witness that when the infamous extermination order was issued by the governor of the state of Missouri, and when twelve thousand defenseless citizens who had done no wrong were exiled from their homes, they sought refuge elsewhere and then formal redress of the injustices done against them through the courts of the land, even to the president of the United States. We did not then urge our people to revolt against unjust persecution, corrupt public officials, or their civil government, but to seek redress through constitutional means. We urge the same process for all minorities today.

6. *We encourage our Church members to vote, to seek out good, wise, and honest men for public office, and to assume an active part in their community to improve it.* The historic position of the Church has been one that is concerned with the quality of man's contemporary environment as well as preparing him for eternity. In fact, as social and political conditions affect man's behavior now, they obviously affect eternity.

The growing worldwide responsibilities of the Church make it inadvisable for the Church to seek to respond to all the various and complex issues involved in the mounting problems of the many cities and communities in which members live. But this complexity does not absolve members as individuals from filling their responsibilities as citizens in their own communities.

We urge our members to do their civic duty and to assume their responsibilities as individual citizens in seeking solutions to the problems which beset our cities and communities.

With our wide-ranging mission, so far as mankind is concerned, Church members cannot ignore the many practical problems that require solution if our families are to live in an environment conducive to spirituality. Where solutions to these practical problems require cooperative action with those not of our faith, members should not be reticent in doing their part in joining and leading in those efforts where they can make an individual contribution to those causes which are consistent with the standards of the Church. Individual Church members cannot, of course, represent or commit the Church, but should, nevertheless, be "anxiously engaged" in good causes, using the principles of the gospel of Jesus Christ as their constant guide.

7. *The Church has urged its members to be efficient users of our resources and to avoid waste and pollution, and to clean up their own immediate environment, or that over which they have control.* It was Goethe who said, "Let everyone sweep in front of his own door and the whole world will be clean." We have made an appeal to all Church members to clean up their premises, to plant gardens and trees, and then to use efficiently what they grow. We have found that Church members have responded well to this appeal, thus becoming more self-reliant and responsibly concerned for their neighbors and their environment.

8. *Above all, we urge our Church members to heed strictly the commandments of God, particularly the Ten Commandments, for their happiness, peace, and prosperity.* Again, we reiterate that it is the belief of our people that as long as we regard God as our Sovereign and uphold His laws, we shall be free from bondage and protected from external danger.

We have not yet reached the diseases that are destroying our political, social, economic, and religious lives, and that will, if not reached, destroy our civilization that has been thousands of years in building.

Furthermore, we shall not reach the diseases till we get back to the precepts of Sinai and the teachings of Christ our Lord. There is no other way than this. And here we may return to the words of Jesus to the Pharisee: "Thou shalt love the Lord thy God with all thy heart, and with all thy soul, and with all thy mind. This is the first and great commandment. And the second is like unto it, Thou shalt love thy neighbour as thyself. On these two commandments hang all the law and the prophets." (Matthew 23:37-40.)

These are the sovereign remedies for the diseases that are now eating away the vitals of our political, social, economic, and religious lives, and that are destroying our civilization.

John Greenleaf Whittier penned:

> ". . . where's the manly spirit
> of the true-hearted and the unshackled gone?
>
> "Sons of old freemen, do we but inherit
> Their names alone?
>
> "Is the old Pilgrim spirit quenched within us,
> Stoops the strong manhood of our souls so low,
> That Mammon's lure or Party's wile can win us
>   To silence now?
>
> "Now, when our land to ruin's brink is verging,
> In God's name, let us speak while there is time!
> Now, when the padlocks for our lips are forging,
> Silence is crime!"
>   —"A Summons"

Because of love for our great country, we speak out "while there is time." We implore God, who has so graciously granted to us our freedoms and prosperity, to preserve our land and give wisdom to our nation's leadership and spiritual strength to this nation's people.

We urge all to repent of our common sins and recast our own lives to fit the example and teachings of the Master. For we stand today not too far from where Lincoln stood during some of the darkest days of the Civil War, when in a proclamation for a national fast day, March 30, 1863, he said:

"We have been the recipients of the choicest bounties of Heaven. We have been preserved, these many years, in peace and prosperity. We have grown in numbers, wealth, and power as no other nation has ever grown; but we have forgotten God. We have forgotten the gracious hand which preserved us in peace, and multiplied and enriched and strengthened us; and we have vainly imagined, in the deceitfulness of our hearts, that all these blessings were produced by some superior wisdom and virtue of our own. Intoxicated with unbroken success, we have become too self-sufficient to feel the necessity of redeeming and preserving grace, too proud to pray to the God that made us."

May God grant us time to rectify ourselves as a people and a nation before Him and thus merit His approval and benediction upon us all.

VIII

The Price of Liberty: Eternal Vigilance

"The greatest threat to the freedom of any nation is erosion—not erosion from the soil, but erosion of the national morality and character. What we have to fear is not force from without, but weakness from within."

The dictum of Curran seems appropriate as a theme, that "the price of liberty is eternal vigilance." Freedom is an eternal principle. Heaven disapproves of force, coercion, and intimidation. Only a free people can be truly a happy people. Of all sad things in the world, the saddest is to see a people who have once known liberty and freedom and then lost it.

I have seen the unquenchable yearning of the human heart for liberty on two unforgettable occasions. These experiences are indelibly etched on the memory of my soul.

I saw this yearning spirit in the faces of many European people, in the aftermath of World War II. It fell my lot, under the direction of the president of the Church, to be among the first to go into war-torn European countries and distribute food, clothing, and bedding to the suffering members of our church. I saw firsthand entire nations prostrate, flat on their backs economically. I looked into the face of hunger—the pale, the thin, the many dressed in rags, and some barefoot. I saw the refugees, the poor unwanted souls who were driven from their homes to destinations unknown. They came with all their possessions on their backs. I visited some of their homes—shacks—where as many as twenty-two people were living in one room. I saw men enslaved by habit barter their food and clothing for a cigarette. I saw some who were fortunate to get hold of an American magazine and pour over its pages and wonder if what they saw could possibly be true. I saw the struggles on every hand to get to America—some legal and others illegal—all in an effort to enjoy freedom and liberty. These were a people who had once known freedom, but had let it slip away.

The second unforgettable experience was when I was in Russia in 1959. We had been touring seven European countries as a part of the objective of the government of the United States to develop world markets and create good will.

Mr. Khrushchev had promised me that I would be able to visit a Christian church in Russia. During our stay there, the guides did everything possible to prevent this. On the way to the airport, before leaving Moscow, I insisted that we go to a Baptist Church in Moscow. It was only a few minutes out of the way. Reluctantly, we were taken to the church. Our guides had told us that the churches were empty, that no one attended church any more, and that religion is the "opiate of the people."

When we arrived at that Baptist Church, we found it full to overflowing. I looked into the faces of the people. Many were middle-aged and older, but a surprising number were young. As we were being ushered to pews, which had been vacated for our unexpected visit, people reached out and grasped for our hands to touch us, "almost," in the words of one newsman, "as one would reach out for the last final caress of one's most beloved just before the casket is lowered." They were in misery and yet a light shone through the misery. They gripped our hands like frightened children.

Later in the service I was asked to address the congregation. I spoke to them about God and Jesus Christ, His Son. I encouraged them to be unafraid and to pray for peace. I witnessed to them the reality of the resurrection and that this life is only a part of eternity. Then, in closing, I told them that truth would endure and that time was on the side of truth.

I don't recall all I said, but I recall being lifted up and inspired by their rapt faces. When I sat down, the whole congregation broke into a favorite hymn of my childhood, "God Be with You Till We Meet Again." We walked down the aisle and they waved their handerchiefs in farewell—it seemed all 1500 were waving. When we finally left, the young lady Russian guide whispered to my wife, "I'm a Christian, too."

It has been my privilege to speak before many church bodies in all parts of the world, but the impact of that experience is almost indescribable. I shall never forget that evening as long as I live.

Seldom, if ever, have I felt the oneness of mankind and the unquenchable yearning of the human heart for freedom so keenly as at that moment. One correspondent described the experience in these words: "The Communist plan is that when these 'last believers' die off, religion will die with them. What the atheists don't know is that God can't be stamped out either by legislated atheism or firing squad. This Methodist back-slider who occasionally grumbles about having to go to church, stood crying unashamedly, throat lumped, and chills running from spine to toes. It was the most heart-rending and most inspiring scene I've ever witnessed. With heavy hearts we left to rejoin the smug, smart-aleck atheist guides who took us to the church but refused to go in." (Tom Anderson, *Farm and Ranch Magazine*.)

Never will I forget this victory of spirit over tyranny, oppression, and ignorance. Never can I doubt the ultimate deliverance of the Russian people.

Freedom from aggression is a justifiable concern. As historians have pointed out, however, great nations do not usually fall by external aggression; they first erode and decay inwardly, so that, like rotten fruit, they fall of themselves.

The history of nations shows that the cycle of the body politic slowly but surely undergoes change. It progresses—
—From bondage to spiritual faith
—From spiritual faith to courage
—From courage to freedom
—From freedom to abundance
—From abundance to selfishness
—From selfishness to complacency
—From complacency to apathy
—From apathy to fear
—From fear to dependency
—From dependency to bondage

The greatest threat to the freedom of any nation is erosion—not erosion of the soil, but erosion of the national morality and character. What we have to fear is not force from without, but weakness from within.

Every nation yearns for liberty, but too frequently its own self-indulgence precludes the possibility of freedom. I speak of the trend of pleasure without conscience, wealth without work, business without morality, politics without principle, and worship without sacrifice. I believe personally there is a strong relationship between a strong, prosperous nation and the faith and righteousness of its people.

There are indispensable conditions that must be met if a nation is to preserve freedom and prevent its own downfall. May I cite four of these conditions—pillars upon which a nation's security rests.

1. *A faith in God and in the universal brotherhood of all mankind.*

I believe with all my heart the words of the American patriot Patrick Henry, who, on the eve of the American Revolution, said,

"There is a just God who presides over the destinies of nations and who will raise up friends to fight our battles for us." Further, it is part of my faith that no people can maintain freedom unless their political institutions are founded on faith in God and belief in the existence of moral law. God has endowed men with certain inalienable rights, and no government may morally limit or destroy these.

The Founding Fathers of the United States seemed to have a clear realization that, to survive, the new nation would need a reliance on the protection of God for their survival. In the Declaration of Independence there is an appeal to the "Supreme Judge of the world" and to "the laws of nature and nature's God." The document concludes with this affirmation: "And for support of this Declaration, with a firm reliance on the Protection of Divine Providence, we mutually pledge to each other our Lives, our Fortunes, and our Sacred Honor."

Here we see that the principle of supremacy of the individual over government is rooted in religious precept. The corollary to this recognition and reliance upon God is the belief in the worth of the individual. The two precepts go hand in hand. The truth is very evident and simple. There is a God in heaven who is the sovereign power of the universe, and we are His literal offspring. He has endowed us with inalienable rights, among which are life, liberty, and the pursuit of happiness. This He has implanted in the human breast. This is why men cannot be driven indefinitely or led by despotic rulers to intellectual or physical slavery and bondage. Fear and despotism may rule for a generation or two, or three, but in time the human spirit rebels, the spirit of liberty manifests itself, and its tyrannous hand is overthrown. Yes, as the offspring of God, we share a common paternity that makes us literally brothers, and thus a common destiny. When this truth sinks into the human heart, men demand their rights—life, liberty, and happiness. It is as the apostle Paul told the Corinthians, "Where the Spirit of the Lord is, there is liberty." (2 Corinthians 3:17.)

I believe this spirit of liberty is beginning to manifest itself in Soviet Russia today, as evidenced by the testimonial of the Nobel Prize recipient, Alexander Solzhenitsyn:

"We dissidents in the U.S.S.R. don't have any tanks, we don't have any weapons, we have no organization. We don't have anything. Our hands are empty; we have only a heart and what we have lived through in the last half century under this system. When we have found the firmness within ourselves to stand up for our rights, we have done so. It's only by our firmness of spirit that we have withstood, and I'm standing here before you, not because of the kindness or the good will of Communism, not thanks to détente, but thanks to my own firmness and your firm support.

"The Communists knew that I would not give up one inch, not one hair, and when they couldn't do more, they themselves fell back. This was taught to me by the difficulties of my own life." (*U.S. News and World Report,* July 14, 1975, p. 49.)

In the meantime, we must not forget the source of all our blessings—our prosperity, our wealth, our comforts, our freedom. We must not forget that it is by God's gracious hand that these blessings are preserved, and not by our own superior wisdom. May we keep alive our faith in God by worshiping Him and keeping His commandments.

2. *Strong homes and family ties.*

The home is the rock foundation, the cornerstone of civilization. No nation will rise above its homes, and no nation will long endure when the family unit is weakened or destroyed. I need not remind you of the great threat to the family in all nations of the world today. Divorce is epidemic. The father's place at the head of the home is being challenged, and mothers have, in many instances, left the hearth to join the work force, thus weakening the stability of the home. Children, not growing up with strong parental guidance and spiritual influence, are allowed to roam freely. Not only does this lack of training and permissiveness sponsor indolence, but many of these youth, out of boredom, have also turned to drugs, juvenile delinquency, or crime.

3. *A political climate and governmental system that protects man's inalienable rights.*

Every governmental system has a sovereign, one or several who possess all the executive, legislative, and judicial powers. That sovereign may be an individual, a group, or the people themselves. Broadly speaking, there are only two governmental systems in the world today. One system recognizes that the sovereign power is vested in the head of state (a monarchy or dictatorship) or a group of men (an oligarchy). This system is as old as history and rests on the premise that the ruler grants to the people the rights and powers he thinks they should have. It is the basis of Roman or civil law, and all dictatorships of history. The system is wrong regardless of how benevolent the dictator may be, because it denies that which belongs to all men inalienably—their right to life, property, and liberty. Since all men are brothers, it follows that "it is not right that any man should be in bondage one to another." (D&C 101:79.)

The other system is that which had its historic origin in 1776, the year of the American independence. The Founding Fathers were men who understood the tyranny that can come out of the system of civil law. They had been indoctrinated in a different system of thought, that of common law, which is premised on the idea that true sovereignty rests with the people. Believing this to be in accord with truth, they inserted this imperative in the Declaration of Independence: "That to secure these Rights [life, liberty, and the pursuit of happiness], Governments are instituted among Men, deriving their just Powers from the Consent of the Governed."

Later, when the young nation had won her independence through the Revolutionary War, a free peoples' representative drafted a second document, the Constitution of the United States, which opens with this Preamble:

"We, the people of the United States, in order to form a more perfect Union, establish justice, insure domestic tranquillity, provide for the common defense, promote the general welfare, and secure the blessings of liberty to ourselves and our posterity, do ordain and establish this Constitution for the United States of America."

Here the people were speaking. They recognized their sovereignty, not that of a king, emperor, or oligarchy. All rights and powers not granted specifically to the government were retained by themselves. This is the difference between freedom and despotism!

There are only two possible sources of man's rights. Rights are either God-given as part of the divine plan or they are granted by government as part of the political plan. Reason, necessity, tradition, and religious convictions all lead me to accept the divine origin of these rights. If we accept the premise that human rights are granted by government, then we must be willing to accept the corollary that they can be denied by government. I, for one, shall never accept that premise. As the French political economist, Frederick Bastiat, phrased it so succinctly, "Life, liberty, and property do not exist because men have made laws. On the contrary, it was the fact that life, liberty, and property existed beforehand that caused men to make laws in the first place." (*The Law,* 1850, p. 6.)

Since God created man with certain inalienable rights, and man, in turn, created government to help secure and safeguard those rights, it follows that man is superior to government and should remain master over it, not the other way around. Even the nonbeliever can appreciate the logic of this relationship. It just isn't good for government to do for people what they can and should do for themselves. Any country that pursues policies that cause the self-reliance, initiative, and freedom of its people to slowly drain away is a country in danger. Let it be remembered that as government leaders our primary task is to protect the freedom of the people.

4. *Elected government officials who are wise and good, and a vigilant, informed citizenry.*

You will note that I have qualified what, to me, should epitomize those fit to lead. They must be both *good* and *wise.* Some men are good, but too naive to be wise statesmen. Other men possess great intellect, but are not morally good. A nation, to endure, must have leaders at the helm whose mandate is higher than the ballot box.

If a government is really the sum of its people, and they are sovereign, then it follows that they must be watchful, vigilant, and informed lest their liberties become gradually usurped by naive or unscrupulous leaders and they awaken to find their liberty gone. Despotism does not arise on the platform of totalitarianism or anything resembling it. It is voted into office on platitudes of "democracy," "freedom," promises of what the government will provide the people, or "something for nothing." In reality, government should do nothing economically for a people that they can do for themselves. To pursue policies to the contrary weakens national initiative and destroys character, and politicians who prey on the gullibilities of the electorate to stay in public office are unworthy of the trust given to them.

We must keep the people informed that collectivism, another word for socialism, is a part of the communist strategy. Communism is essentially socialism. Alexis de Tocqueville, with unusual insight, was able to foresee and predict the spiritual deterioration that would occur if the people forfeited their rights to a paternalistic welfare state:

"After having thus successively taken each member of the community in its powerful grasp, and fashioned him at will, the supreme power then extends its arm over the whole community. It covers the surface of society with a network of small complicated rules, minute and uniform, through which the most original minds and the most energetic characters cannot penetrate, to rise above the crowd. The will of man is not shattered, but softened, bent, and guided: men are seldom forced by it to act, but they are constantly restrained from acting: such a power does not destroy, but it prevents existence; it does not tyrannize, but it compresses, enervates, extinguishes, and stupefies a people, till each nation is reduced to be nothing better than a flock of timid and industrial animals, of which government is the shepherd." (*Democracy in America,* New Rochelle, New York: Arlington House, 2:338.)

Wise leaders ought to have, then, as one of their major objectives, the education of citizens to the truth. "Enlighten the people generally," said Thomas Jefferson, "and tyranny and oppression will vanish like evil spirits at the dawn of day." (*Works,* 6:592.)

These, then, are the pillars upon which any nation's national security rests:

1. Faith in God and in the universal brotherhood of all mankind.

2. Strong homes and family ties.

3. A political climate and governmental system that protects man's inalienable rights.

4. Elected government officials who are wise and good, and a vigilant, informed citizenry.

Today we are in a worldwide battle, the first of its kind in history between two opposing systems, freedom and slavery; between the spirit of Christianity and the spirit of the antichrist for the bodies and souls of men. May God grant that we will win the battle by alertness, by determination, by courage, and by an energizing realization of the danger.

The price of liberty is eternal vigilance. Are we willing to pay the price? The days ahead are sobering and challenging and will demand the faith, prayers, and loyalty of all men to the truth. As the ancient apostle declared: "The night is far spent, the day is at hand: let us therefore cast off the works of darkness, and let us put on the armour of light." (Romans 13:12.)

May God give us the wisdom to recognize the danger of complacency, the threat to our freedom, and the strength to meet this danger courageously.

IX

America's Hope

"If we are to survive as an independent, sovereign nation, we must, as free Americans, follow sound economic and political policies, uphold and protect our hallowed Constitution, and live to the letter the virtues of frugality, integrity, loyalty, patriotism, and morality."

As Americans, we share a serious citizenship responsibility. The Prophet Joseph Smith declared, "It is our duty to concentrate all our influence to make popular that which is sound and good, and unpopular that which is unsound." (*History of the Church* 5:286.)

God has told us, in modern scripture, that the United States Constitution was divinely inspired for the specific purpose of eliminating bondage and the violation of the rights and protection that belong to "all flesh." (D&C 101:77-80.) If we believe in God and His works, it is up to each one of us to uphold and defend our Constitution, which guarantees our precious freedom. For God states unequivocally: "Let not that which I have appointed be polluted by mine enemies, by the consent of those who call themselves after my name; For this is a very sore and grievous sin against me, and against my people, in consequence of those things which I have decreed and which are soon to befall the nations." (D&C 101:97-98.)

President David O. McKay declared: "No greater immediate responsibility rests upon members of the Church, upon all citizens of this Republic and of neighboring Republics than to protect the freedom vouchsafed by the Constitution of the United States." (*Conference Report*, April 1950, p. 37.)

As Americans, we have marched a long way down the soul-destroying road of socialism, atheism, and totalitarianism. It is the price we pay when we turn away from God and turn to government to do everything for us. It is the formula by which nations become enslaved by their own leaders.

As England's Lord Acton so succinctly put it, "Power tends to corrupt—but absolute power corrupts absolutely." (*Essays on Freedom and Power*, p. 364.)

Increasing numbers of Americans are subscribing to the myth that you can get something for nothing—as long as the government is footing the bill. In fact, they believe it is the duty of government to take care of them, from the womb to the tomb.

There is no such thing as a free lunch. Everything we get from the government, we pay for in debilitating taxes. Everything the government *gives* to the people, it must first *take* from the people. This is something few Americans appear to understand.

We tend to forget how America became the greatest, most prosperous, and most powerful nation in the world, blessed with an abundance of everything needed for the good life. It didn't just happen. It wasn't an accident. It was all an integral part, I believe, of the divine plan for America. In the early frontier days of this country, a special breed of men and women came here from all over the world, seeking not only opportunity but freedom. They were strong, proud, and fiercely independent. They believed that the surest helping hand was at the end of their own sleeves. They shared one thing in common— an unshakable faith in God and in themselves. And that, without doubt, is the secret of success as viable today as it was yesterday.

With little but raw courage and indomitable purpose, those intrepid pioneers set forth into the unknown by covered wagon, on horseback, and sometimes on foot. The land demanded iron men with steel in their backbones. Nature did the weeding out. But they didn't whine or bleat because things were tough. They asked no favors from any man. They knew what they were up against, and they accepted the challenge. All they wanted was to be left alone to do what had to be done. They were wrenching a civilization out of the wilderness.

America soon blossomed into a rich, fertile, productive nation. Individual initiative—free enterprise—paid off, and American ingenuity flourished in a climate of freedom. Very soon our technology, our inventiveness, and our business know-how became the envy of the world. America had reached maturity, a giant among nations, a glowing example of free enterprise in action, and a perfect demonstration of what free men can do when they are left alone to do it.

But as those affluent years slipped by, voices were heard in the land, singing the siren songs of socialism. And many Americans tapped their feet to the beat of the music. Politicians were already promising something for nothing, that elusive free lunch. Thus, gradually the people let the government infringe upon their precious freedoms, and the preliminary signs of decay began to appear in our young republic.

A current example of this moral erosion can be seen in the food stamp program today. Originally intended to assist those who were on minimum subsistence by drawing on government surpluses being stored at a cost of a million dollars a day, surpluses that had accumulated by government bungling, this program has burgeoned to the extent that today one of every thirteen Americans is drawing food stamps, and one out of every four has been made eligible, by recent legislation. And who pays for all of this? We do—the taxpayers. There is no such thing as a free lunch.

Today, as government becomes increasingly dominant in our affairs, we are becoming more and more like ancient Rome before it crumbled and collapsed. We are choosing bread and circuses instead of facing the challenges that always test a free people. We are no longer the proud leader of the world. We have lost the respect of almost every country, and I know because I've traveled in those countries. Through our policies of equivocation and our politics of expediency and appeasement, we have lost respect. We think we are buying world peace. This is not diplomacy, it is national suicide! No wonder we have earned the contempt of our enemies, who are only too happy to take our money, our food, our industrial equipment, and our technical expertise.

Despite what many say and think, the cold war continues today and during this period of detente. One of the main weapons in the cold-war arsenal of our enemies is inflation.

Our economic situation is extremely serious. The facts are harsh and cold. This is a grim topic. But how can one soften the truth? Inflation, like an insidious disease, is weakening us as a nation. We are in this position because we have lost our national pride and our sense of independence and have sacrificed basic economic principles. When we want something, we go crawling to the government instead of doing it ourselves. We have exchanged those God-inspired principles upon which this once mighty nation was built for a mess of shoddy values. No wonder our structures of freedom are cracking.

Many voices in government today are blaming businessmen, the unions, and even the buying public for not practicing thrift and economy in their shopping habits. The blame for inflation must be laid directly at the door of the federal government itself! Inflation is an increase in the nation's money supply—an increase, to be more exact, in the supply of money and credit. Inflation is *not* caused by rising prices and wages. To the contrary, rising prices and wages, as any solid economist knows, are the direct result of inflation. It stands to reason that when the money supply is increased, all money automatically becomes less valuable. This includes, of course, our savings.

So when our dollars shrink in value, businessmen naturally raise their price tags, and then their employees demand higher wages. You can see how it all becomes a vicious circle.

In a free society such as ours, only the federal government can cause inflation. And the reason it puts more money into circulation is to finance its disastrous policies of deficit spending. As the federal government promotes more and more costly and unnecessary programs, it spends far more than it receives. In order to keep in business, the government has to borrow. To do this, it offers bonds, which are purchased mainly by private banks. Many of these bonds are resold to the Federal Reserve. The Federal Reserve then issues newly printed paper money—or issues credit to pay for the bonds. Thus, new money is created, the money supply is increased, and the value of *all* money is reduced.

It is well to remember that continued government deficits cause inflation; inflation is used as an excuse for ineffective price controls; price controls lead to shortages; and artificial shortages inevitably are used as an excuse to implement rationing. When will we learn these basic economic principles?

The prophet Isaiah wrote: "Therefore my people are gone into captivity, because they have no knowledge." (Isaiah 5:13.)

It is quite obvious that a lack of knowledge and understanding on the part of Americans regarding the causes of inflation, which threatens our economic survival, could well lead us into captivity.

Americans could halt inflation today by demanding that their government stop increasing the supply of money. It is not that the government does not know how to do it—it doesn't want to do it. The excuse is that if it stops printing money, the nation will be plunged into a recession or worse—a depression precipitating an unacceptable percentage of unemployment. But the longer we delay sound action, the more it will cost our nation and its people.

Unfortunately, the average American knows very little about the complexities of economics. He leaves that to the "expertise" of those in government. But the tragedy is that the political spendthrifts in government are the ones who are wrecking our economy. They are spending billions of dollars on useless domestic programs and squandering billions more in support of communist governments that are getting "most favored nation" treatment.

The Congress has failed us abysmally in its historic role as watchdog over our national interests. It could and should put the clamps on irresponsible government spending. Unhappily, when a government embarks on a course of inflation, it must accelerate that inflation in order to perpetuate the false stimulating effect.

If the government were genuinely concerned about full employment and real prosperity, it could do much in bringing it about. It could support the proven and successful free market system, the law of supply and demand, where the buying public, not the government, is the deciding factor in what shall be produced and marketed, including energy products. The bureaucrats ignore the lessons of American history that freedom works and that the ability of individuals to come to mutually beneficial agreements is the very essence of a free society.

There is no problem at all about how to *stop* inflation. The problem is not economic—it's political.

Our original monetary system as established by the Founding Fathers, and the only one authorized by the Constitution, makes this imperative by the following clause: "No state shall . . . make anything but gold and silver coin a tender in payment of debts." (Article 1, Section 10.)

The government is manipulating our monetary system, and unless we return to fiscal responsibility, we can look forward to a highly dangerous economic crisis.

If we are to beat inflation effectively, four vital steps must be taken:

1. Abolish wage and price controls permanently.

2. Stop all spending in excess of tax receipts and make annual payments on the debt.

3. Abrogate all extravagant and unnecessary government programs.

4. Reestablish the gold and silver standard.

Congress has the power and the responsibility to accomplish these measures. If our representatives and senators persist in shirking their duties in this regard, then we'll continue on the same course to economic disaster, and we'll end up with a controlled economy under a totalitarian form of government.

I have seen with my own eyes the end result of continuing inflation. I paid six billion marks for breakfast in Cologne, Germany, in December 1923. That was fifteen cents in American money.

Our spiraling national debt is but one of the danger signs, and is indicative of the culpable negligence of those in the highest echelons of government.

Thomas Jefferson counseled: "To preserve our independence, we must not let our rulers load us with perpetual debt. We must take our choice between economy and liberty, or profusion and servitude." Indeed, paying our debts, or living within our means, was always one of the sterling characteristics of Americans. We looked upon it as a duty to ourselves as individuals and as children of God. Students of history know that no government in the history of mankind has ever created any wealth. People who work create wealth.

God has prospered this land. Though the United States has only about six percent of the world population and seven percent of the land area, our gross national product is about forty percent of the world total. It exceeds that of all other western European countries combined and is three times greater than that of the entire Far East. (1974 *Associated Press Almanac.*)

The United States is the most generous nation under heaven. We have put out 25 billion dollars' worth of food aid around the world— 84 percent of the world's food aid in the past several years.

Some say the free enterprise system is heartless and insensitive to the needs of those less fortunate individuals who are found in any society, no matter how affluent. What about the lame, the sick, and the destitute? Most other countries in the world have attempted to use the power of government to meet this need. Yet, in every case forced charity through government bureaucracies has resulted in the long run in creating more misery, more poverty, and certainly less freedom than when government first stepped in. Charity can be charity only when it is voluntary, and it will be effective only when it is voluntary.

As Henry Grady Weaver wrote in his excellent book *The Mainspring of Human Progress,* "Most of the major ills of the world have been caused by well-meaning people who ignored the principle of individual freedom except as applied to themselves, and who were obsessed with fanatical zeal to improve the lot of mankind-in-mass through some pet formula of their own. . . . The harm done by ordinary criminals, murderers, gangsters, and thieves is negligible in comparison with the agony inflicted upon human beings by the professional 'do-gooders,' who attempt to set themselves up as gods on earth and who would ruthlessly force their views on all others— with the abiding assurance that the end justifies the means." (Pp. 40-41.)

By comparison, America traditionally has relied on individual action and voluntary charity. The result is that the United States has fewer cases of genuine hardship per capita than any other country in the entire world or throughout all history. Even during the depression of the 1930s, Americans ate and lived better than most people in other countries do today.

As Americans, citizens of the greatest nation under heaven, we face difficult days. Never since the days of the Civil War has this choice nation faced such a crisis. Throughout history, great civilizations have disappeared. In every case the pattern bears a grim similarity. First comes a decline in spiritual values, then a repudiation of economic and moral principles of integrity and responsibility, followed by the inevitable loss of freedom.

If we are to survive as an independent, sovereign nation, we must, as free Americans, follow sound economic and political policies, uphold and protect our hallowed Constitution, and live to the letter the virtues of frugality, integrity, loyalty, patriotism, and morality. Today, more than ever before, we need God's influence and guidance in every area of our lives.

America has a spiritual foundation. Her wellsprings are religious. Our crisis is a crisis of faith; our need is for greater spirituality and a return to the basic concepts upon which this nation was established. How much this country needs men with a mandate higher than the ballot box! How much this country needs men in government who acknowledge their debt to the Almighty, men whose lives are a daily witness to the truth of the American motto, "In God We Trust"!

The days ahead are sobering and challenging, and will require the faith, prayers, and loyalty of every American citizen. Our challenge is to keep America strong and free—strong socially, strong economically, and above all, strong spiritually, if our way of life is to endure. Indeed, it is America's only hope for life, liberty, and the pursuit of happiness!

X

The Case for the Free Market

"Our major danger is that we are . . . transferring responsibility from the individual, local, and state governments to the federal government. . . . We cannot long pursue this present trend without its bringing us to national insolvency."

Today it seems evident that we are rearing a generation of Americans who do not understand the productive base of our society and how we came by such prosperity. Evidence of this fact is found in surveys taken among some of our high school and college students, the majority of whom, it is reported, believe private enterprise is a failure, although they don't have a clear understanding of what private enterprise is. With them, as with many adults, there is a vague notion that it is some unfair system that tends to give special advantage to big corporations and wealthy individuals.

From a study done by the Joint Council of Economic Education in 1973, 50 percent of the high school students interviewed could not distinguish between collectivism and a free enterprise society. Fifty percent did not know the United States economy was based on free enterprise. From another study done by the Opinion Research Corporation, the median estimate of the U.S. public was that corporate profits are 28 percent of the sales dollar. Actually, profits are four to five percent.

These attitudes may be the result of the propaganda of certain textbook writers who hold the idea, in many instances, that a planned economy is the remedy for all of our economic ills and the weaknesses in our American way of life, to which they readily point, without referring to the beneficent fruits of the system.

Before a welfare state can flourish, a welfare state mentality must take root. Are we not today yielding the harvest of seeds sown from the days of the Great Depression to the present? The ethic of today seems calculated to indoctrinate our citizenry toward a dependency on the state. Our Founding Fathers recognized that certain rights were inalienable, that is, God-given; today, the state is being looked to as the guarantor of human rights—life, liberty, and property. Our forebears practiced the biblical ethic that man should earn his bread by the sweat of his *own* brow; today's ethic seems to be that it is right to be supported by the sweat of *another's* brow.

I ask, Where are the exponents of the free market today? Who is speaking out for the philosophy and system that has brought about America's greatness and prosperity? You will not find free market exponents among the majority in the halls of Congress, nor in government bureaucracies, nor in labor, the pulpit, or the classroom. Paradoxically, they are not any more heard among the majority of businessmen. Many businessmen kowtow to the power of governmental regulatory agencies; others have their hand out to the federal trough. The platforms of the two great political parties in our land are contradictory to a free man's political and economic philosophy. The majority party is unabashedly pro-collectivist; the minority party offers a more gradual interventionism as an alternative. My intent, in this chapter, is to plead the case for the free market in a way that, hopefully, the average citizen may understand.

To illustrate my point, let me relate a parable that contrasts two different philosophies.

Two fathers lived side by side as neighbors. Each had two sons. Each had a good job, a roomy house, and material means to provide the best of life's luxuries. The essential difference between the two fathers was one of philosophy.

Mr. A's objective with his sons was to instill principles that would bring about self-respect, personal responsibility, and independence. His method merits our scrutiny.

When his boys were young, he taught them how to work at simple tasks by his side. When they became more mature, he developed a work-incentive program. The pay scale was commensurate with the quality of the work performed. An "average job," for example, paid fifty cents; "above average," sixty cents; "exceptional," seventy-five cents. A "one-dollar job" was the impossible task, a goal that he soon observed the boys were striving after. He impressed on them that the only limitations to their earnings were their own personal initiative and desire. He emphasized the necessity of postponing wants so they could save for the future. The lessons were well learned over a period of time.

There was an undergirding moral element to Mr. A's philosophy, a principle more "caught" than taught. A simple example will suffice. One day the boys, now young men, were working in his plant. Mr. A. observed some sloppy work being done on one of the products. He asked to see the product, and removed the label. One of the boys resisted. "Why are you doing that, Dad?" he asked. Mr. A. replied, "I'll not have my name attached to a shoddy product. When my name goes on, my customers must know I've given them my best workmanship. Would you want to own this product?" It was an answer that provided a lesson that would last a lifetime. How could the Golden Rule be emphasized more effectively in business!

Mr. B also had a philosophy, albeit one that was reactionary to the early struggles of youth. "I'll not have my kids go through what I did." His philosophy was designed to remove the struggle from life. His method also merits our consideration.

Regularly his sons were provided with generous allowances. Little work was expected in their formative years. In later years the boys were encouraged to work, but now they were too comfortable in their security. After all, they had all their material wants satisfied. At this juncture Mr. B. made a profound discovery: *wants always exceed needs and are never satisfied unless disciplined.* To counteract the lack of self-discipline, Mr. B. embarked on a routine of imposed restraints. To his chagrin, he found his sons embittered toward him, ungrateful, and frequently disobedient to rules imposed on them.

Need I draw conclusions from this parable? Is it not apparent which philosophy develops a productive, contributive member of society and which philosophy sponsors dependency? Is it not also apparent which philosophy will best prepare one for emotional or economic crises?

I do not apologize for the simplicity of the illustration. One may argue that the characters are exaggerated, but even a child can understand the effects of Mr. B's caretaker philosophy. Is not his philosophy analagous in many ways to the government official who argues, "In this country welfare is no longer charity, it is a right. More and more Americans feel that their government owes them something"? (*U.S. News and World Report*, April 21, 1975, p. 49.)

But it is not Mr. B's philosophy that commands our attention here; it is Mr. A's. Why is it that the elements in his philosophy are so unfamiliar to so many that they believe their government owes them something? Our task is to make Mr. A's philosophy both familiar and credible. When it is understood *and believed*, it will be defended with the same vigor and determination that made our Founding Fathers pledge their lives, their fortunes, and their sacred honor.

Many view the idea of the free-enterprise or free-market system as only an alternative economic system to other systems. This is a serious oversight and causes many to miss the most crucial elements in the free-market system.

First: The free-market system rests on a moral base. Before one can appreciate why this premise is true, two questions must be answered: What is man?, and From what source does man derive his rights?

Our governmental system, like the systems of ancient Israel and biblical Christianity, recognizes man as a special creation of God. He is not, as some theorists reason, a product of chance or merely an educated animal. His paternal origin is from God. Thus, man inherently possesses God-implanted attributes and potential: reason, free agency, judgment, compassion, initiative, and a personal striving for perfection.

Thus we see that the principle of supremacy of the individual over government is rooted in religious precept. This is why the founders of our nation were so influenced by the writings of John Locke, who declared that man was naturally in a state of perfect freedom, that he had a right to preservation and property, and that the source of all this was God. (See John Locke's treatise, *Of Civil Government.*)

The Founding Fathers recognized that no people can maintain freedom unless their political institutions are founded on faith in God and belief in the existence of moral law. They realized that to survive, this new nation needed a reliance on the protection of God. In the Declaration of Independence we find their appeal to "the Supreme Judge of the world" and to "the Laws of Nature and of Nature's God." The document concludes with their affirmation of "a firm reliance on the Protection of Divine Providence."

The implications of this moral basis to our political-economic system is that God is the dispenser of man's rights, not government. The inalienable right of free choice is implanted in the human breast. Man is born to choose for himself. This is why man cannot be driven indefinitely or led by despotic leaders to intellectual, physical, or economic bondage. Once a person awakens to the truth of his divine identity, he demands his rights: the right to property, the right to make his own decisions, the right to plan his own welfare, and the right to improve himself materially, intellectually, and spiritually.

Second: the free-market is based on the right to property. The right to property is again based on scriptural precept. It recognizes that the earth belongs to the Lord, that He created it for man's blessing and benefit. Thus, man's desire to own property, his own home and goods, his own business, is desirable and good. Utopian and communitarian schemes that eliminate property rights are not only unworkable, they also deny to man his inherent desire to improve his station. They are therefore contrary to the pursuit of happiness.

No property rights! Man's incentive would be diminished to satisfying only his barest necessities such as food and clothing. How this truth is evident in the communist countries today!

No property rights! No incentive to enter individual enterprise, to risk one's own capital, because the fruits of one's labor could not be enjoyed.

No property rights! No contractual relationships to buy and sell since title to possession of goods could not be granted.

No property rights! No recognition of divine law that prohibits man from stealing and coveting others' possessions. One cannot steal that which belongs to everyone, nor can he covet that which is not another's!

No property rights! No possibility of the sanctity of one's own home and the joy that comes from creation, production, and ownership.

A free-market philosophy recognizes property rights as sacred. Because the individual is entitled to ownership of goods and property that he has earned, he is sovereign, so far as human law is concerned, over his own goods. He may retain possession of his goods. He may pass his wealth on to family or to charitable causes.

Charity, that greatest of godly virtues, would never be possible without property rights, for one cannot give what one does not own.

James Madison recognized that property consisted not only of man's external goods—his land, merchandise, or money—but, most sacredly, he had title also to his thoughts, opinions, and conscience. A civil government's obligation, then, is to safeguard this right and to frame laws that secure to every man the free exercise of his conscience and the right and control of his property.

No liberty is possible unless a man is protected in his title to his legal holdings and property and can be indemnified, by the law, for its loss or destruction. Remove this right and man is reduced to serfdom. Former United States Supreme Court Justice George Sutherland said it this way: "To give [man] liberty but take from him the property which is the fruit and badge of his liberty, is to still leave him a slave." (Address to the New York Bar Association, January 21, 1921.)

Third: The free market is based on the right to enjoy private enterprise for profit. As a country we have suffered under half a century of liberal propaganda demeaning economic success. This was done by referring to men who are willing to risk their capital (profit) in tools and equipment as "coupon clippers," "economic royalists," "capitalists," and "profiteers"—as though there were something inherently evil in profit.

Profit is the reward for honest labor. It is the incentive that causes a man to risk his capital to build a business. If he cannot keep or invest that which he has earned, neither may he own, nor will he risk. Profit creates wealth; wealth creates more work opportunity; and more work opportunity creates greater wealth. None of this is possible without incentive.

There is another benefit to profit. It provides man with moral choices. With profit, man can choose to be greedy and selfish; he can invest and expand, thereby providing others with jobs; and he can be charitable. Charity is not charity unless it is voluntary. It cannot be voluntary if there is nothing to give.

Only saved profit, not government, creates more jobs. The only way government can create jobs is to take the money from productive citizens in the form of taxes and transfer it to government programs. Without someone's generating profit that can be taxed, government revenue is not possible.

Fourth: The free market is the right to voluntary exchange of goods and services, free from restraints and controls. Nothing is more to be prized, nor more sacred, than man's free choice. Free choice is the essence of free enterprise. It recognizes that the common man will make choices in his own self-interest. It allows a manufacturer to produce what he wants, how much, and to set his own price. It allows the buyer to decide if he wants a certain product at the price established. It preserves the right to work when and where we choose.

In his first inaugural address, Thomas Jefferson said that the sum of good government shall leave citizens "free to regulate their own pursuits of industry and improvement, and shall not take from the mouth of labor the bread it has earned."

Why does our system produce more bread, manufacture more shoes, and assemble more TV sets than Russian socialism? It does so precisely because our government does *not* guarantee these things. If it did, there would be so many accompanying taxes, controls, regulations, and political manipulations that the productive genius that is America's, based on freedom of choice, would soon be reduced to the floundering level of waste and inefficiency now found behind the Iron Curtain.

When government presumes to demand more and more of the fruits of man's labors through taxation, and reduces more and more his actual income by printing money and furthering debt, the wage earner is left with less and less with which to buy food and to provide housing, medical care, education, and private welfare. Individuals are then left without a choice and must look to the state as the benevolent supporter of these services. When that happens, liberty is gone.

Fifth: A free market survives with competition. Were it not for more competition among goods or services, there could be no standard by which a buyer could discern shoddy merchandise or inept service from excellence. Were it not for competition, the seller could price his goods and services according to his own fancy. It is competition that determines what is good, better, and best. It is competition that determines the price for products or services. If goods are overpriced in comparison with other comparable goods, the buyer will refuse to buy, thus forcing the seller to drop his price.

There is a glaring paradox in our society. On the one hand, legislation has been enacted allegedly to prevent one business or combination of businesses (a monopoly) from disrupting or eliminating competitors in the market. On the other hand, we have yet to awaken fully to the worst form of monopolistic practice currently impeding the free market. I refer to government monopoly, when government either by ownership or regulation prevents the full freedom of action by sellers. This, of course, regulates and controls prices. No better example exists today than the so-called energy crisis.

As a nation, we have artificially regulated the price of natural gas for over twenty years. The Federal Power Commission has set prices and burdened the oil industry with regulations. Consequently, the oil industry has not had the incentive to discover natural gas or drill for oil even though the reserves are there. The environmentalists, with the help of activist lawyers, have combined to make it almost impossible to drill for oil economically. What industry wants to risk its capital fighting through hearings and lawsuits that double and treble its investment costs? So exploration does not take place, or reserves are kept off the market to await the day when government will deregulate. The government is then left with the alternative to go abroad to supply our demand for foreign oil reserves. The most effective energy policy our government could devise would be to step out of the regulatory business. This would provide once again the incentives for industry to make investment and exploration.

Freedom from bureaucratic monopoly is essential to allowing our free market to work effectively. I hope we wake up to this lesson before our freedoms are lost altogether.

We have talked thus far about the vital elements to a free market operation. How does it all work together to bring about needed goods and services? Let me illustrate.

How do our cities and towns each day obtain the quantity of food products they demand? Of all agencies engaged in supplying cities with food, almost none knows how much the city consumes or how much is being produced. Despite this ignorance, the cities receive about the right amount of food needed without great surplus or shortage. How is this accomplished without a central directing body telling each producer what it should produce? The answer, of course, is the operation of the free market—free enterprise in action.

Suppose, for example, that a given city did not receive the amount of food products needed to satisfy its demand. Rather than go without, many people would be willing to pay higher prices. Thus, prices would increase and the volume of production would rise. This would end the shortage. More food would be shipped to that city and less to other places. Or suppose there were an oversupply of food products. To avoid spoilage, the seller must lower his price. This, in turn, would be a signal to the producer to cut back on production. Thus, the oversupply would automatically be regulated. Less food would be shipped to that city and more to other places.

Just as price regulates the distribution of food in a given city, so it also determines the total amount produced in the country. Greater profits provide farmers with incentives to produce given products. If the supply increases at a pace faster than the demand for a product, farmers and ranchers are compelled to lower their prices. As it becomes less profitable to produce, potential producers are deterred from engaging in this occupation, and the unprofitable producers divert to something else or abandon farming altogether.

This is how this remarkable system works in all industries when government and planning control and price fixing are left out, yet few of our citizens seem to understand this. Economic literacy among our people has not been one of the bright spots in our 200-year-old history. Yet it is apparent that when ignorance prevails, the people eventually suffer.

The principles behind our American free market philosophy can be reduced to a rather simple formula. Here it is:

1. Economic security for all is impossible without widespread abundance.

2. Abundance is impossible without industrious and efficient production.

3. Such production is impossible without energetic, willing, and eager labor.

4. Such labor is not possible without incentive.

5. Of all forms of incentive, the freedom to attain a reward for one's labors is the most sustaining for most people. Sometimes called

the profit motive, it is simply the right to plan and to earn and to enjoy the fruits of one's labor.

6. This profit motive diminishes as government controls, regulations, and taxes increase to deny the fruits of success to those who produce.

7. Therefore, any attempt through government intervention to redistribute the material rewards of labor can only result in the eventual destruction of the productive base of society, without which real abundance and security for more than the ruling elite are quite impossible.

Yes, what worked for Mr. A in producing self-disciplined, responsible, contributive sons to society will work for a community; what works for a community will work for a state; and what works for the state will work for this nation—if we as American citizens demand that government officials perform only those duties provided by the Constitution and Bill of Rights.

Examples abound in the world of the failure of alternative systems to the free market. What amazes me is that we cannot see from their example the obvious failure of socialism, what it does to a nation's economy, and how it morally debilitates a people.

Great Britain is a tragic example of this. Here is a nation that has provided the free world with a tradition of freedom and democratic rights, stemming from the Magna Carta and coming down through other important historical documents and statements by famous Englishmen. Yet England today is losing her freedom. She has become a giant welfare state. Today government spending in Great Britain amounts to 60 percent of her national income.

This is socialism. Medical doctors under socialized medicine are leaving Great Britain in record numbers, as are thousands of others.

British Prime Minister James Callaghan said, "We used to think that you could just spend your way out of a recession and increase employment by cutting taxes and boosting government spending. I tell you, in all candor, that that option no longer exists, and that insofar as it ever did exist, it only worked by injecting bigger doses of inflation into the economy, followed by higher levels of unemployment as the next step." (London *Times,* September 29, 1976, from Labor Party Conference at Blackpool, England, p. 4.)

Such a confession led the renowned economist, the Nobel Laureate, Dr. Milton Friedman, to comment, "That must surely rank as one of the most remarkable and courageous statements ever made by a leader of a democratic government. Read it again. Savor it. It is a

confession of the intellectual bankruptcy of the policy that has guided
every British Government in the postwar period—not only Labor
governments but also Tory governments; of the policy that has
guided almost every other Western government—including the U.S.
under both Republican and Democratic administrations; of the policy
that is now being recommended to Mr. Carter by his advisers."
(*Newsweek,* December 6, 1976, p. 87.)

Consider another example: our neighbor to the north, Canada.
For twenty years (1944-1964), the province of Saskatchewan lived
under a socialist government. Here is what the premier, the Honorable W. Ross Thatcher, said about this experience:

> In 1944, the Socialists said they would solve the unemployment problems
> by building government factories. They promised to use the profits to build
> highways, schools, hospitals, and to finance better social welfare measures
> generally. Over the years they set up 22 so-called crown corporations. . . . By the
> time we had taken over the government, . . . 12 of the crown corporations had
> gone bankrupt or been disposed of. Others were kept operating by repeated and
> substantial government grants.
>
> During the whole period the Socialists waged war against private business.
> The making of profits was condemned as an unforgivable sin. What was the
> result? Investors simply turned their backs on the Socialists. Dozens of oil com-
> panies pulled up stakes and moved out. Gas exploration ground to a complete
> halt. Prospecting in our vast north became almost non-existent.
>
> During the period Canada was experiencing the greatest economic boom
> in her history, Saskatchewan received only a handful of new factories. After 18
> years of Socialism, there were fewer jobs in manufacturing than existed in
> 1945—this despite the investment of $500 million in crown corporation. . . .
>
> During the period more than 600 completely new taxes were introduced;
> 650 other taxes were increased. Per capita taxes in Saskatchewan were soon
> substantially out of line with our sister provinces—one more reason why in-
> dustry located elsewhere.
>
> . . . the Socialists promised to make Saskatchewan a Mecca for the working
> man. Instead, we saw the greatest mass exodus of people out of an area since
> Moses led the Jews out of Egypt. Since the war, 270,000 of our citizens left
> Saskatchewan to find employment elsewhere.
>
> If there are any Americans who think that Socialism is the answer, I wish
> they could come to Saskatchewan to study what has happened to our province.
> (Quoted in Corydon, Indiana, *Republican.*)

We say, "It can't happen here." The lesson of New York City
should tells us that this same thing is happening here—to us—*now!*
As Dr. Friedman has pointed out, New York City is no longer
governed by its elected officials. It is governed by a committee of
overseers appointed by the State of New York. New York City has
partially lost its freedom. When will we learn the lesson that fiscal ir-
responsibility leads to a loss of self-government? When will we learn

that when you lose economic independence, you lose political freedom?

We have accepted a frightening degree of socialism in our country. The question is, how much? The amount of freedom depends upon the amount of federal control and spending. A good measurement is to determine the amount, or percentage, of income of the people that is taken over and spent by the state. In Russia, the individual works almost wholly for the state, leaving little for his own welfare. Scandinavia takes about 65 to 70 percent of the income of the people, England some 60 percent. The United States is now approximately 44 percent.

There are indications that America is moving away from the philosophy that made her the most prosperous nation in the world. In effect, we are moving toward the philanthropic philosophy of Mr. B and abandoning the work-incentive philosophy of Mr. A. Mr. B's philosophy has crept in unawares under the guise of a new name—egalitarianism. It is, of course, the socialist doctrine of equality. It strikes a sympathetic chord with many Americans because its initial goal is equality of rights. Today, however, the goal for the proponents of equality is to restructure our entire economic system using the power of the federal government to enforce their grand design. They now advocate throughout our economy that we "redistribute wealth and income," a good definition for socialism. Our present middle-of-the-road policy is, as Von Mises suggested, socialism by the installment plan.

Americans have always been committed to taking care of the poor, aged, and unemployed. We've done this on the basis of Judaic-Christian beliefs and humanitarian principles. It has been fundamental to our way of life that charity must be voluntary if it is to be charity. Compulsory benevolence is not charity. Today's egalitarians are using the federal government to redistribute wealth in our society, not as a matter of voluntary charity, but as a matter of right.

The chief weapon used by the federal government to achieve this equality is through so-called transfer payments. This is a term that simply means that the federal government collects from one income group and transfers payments to another by the tax system. These payments are made in the form of Social Security benefits, housing subsidies, Medicaid, food stamps, to name a few. Today, total cost of such programs exceeds $150 billion dollars. That represents about 42 percent of the total of all government federal spending, or about one dollar out of every seven dollars of personal income. (See *U.S. News and World Report*, August 4, 1975, pp. 32-33.) When will we resolve as Americans that a dollar cannot make the trip to Washington, D.C., and back without a bureaucratic bite being taken out of it?

Medicaid, the government's regular health program for the poor, cost taxpayers $13 billion in 1975. Medicare, the program for the disabled and elderly, cost $15 billion. Aid to families with dependent children cost over $5 billion, and about $3 billion was spent on food stamps. This is to name only a few of the so-called benefits paid out.

Our present Social Security program has been going in the hole at the rate of $12 billion a year, and yet the party now in power wants to increase the benefits to include a comprehensive national health insurance program. Recognizing that the present program will be insolvent by 1985, President Carter has now recommended that Social Security be funded out of the general tax funds. Charges were made in the last election campaign that the Social Security program was going bankrupt. These charges were denied. Now the truth is out. The President's recommendation must be regarded as an admission of the failure of the present system and as a calculated policy to take this country into full-scale socialism.

Our major danger is that we are currently—and have been for forty years—transferring responsibility from the individual, local, and state governments to the federal government, precisely the same course that led to the economic collapse in Great Britain and in New York. We cannot long pursue this present trend without its bringing us to national insolvency.

Edmund Burke, the great British political philosopher, warned of the threat of egalitarianism: "A perfect equality will indeed be produced—that is to say, equal wretchedness, equal beggary, and, on the part of the partitioners, a woeful, helpless, and desperate disappointment. Such is the event of all compulsory equalizations. They pull down what is above; they never raise what is below; and they depress high and low together beneath the level of what was originally the lowest."

All would like to equalize with those who are better off than they themselves. They fail to realize that incomes differ, and will always differ, because people differ in their economic drive and ability. History indicates that governments have been unable to prevent inequality of incomes. Further, equalization efforts stifle initiative and retard progress to the extent that the real incomes of everyone are lowered.

We must remember that government assistance and control are essentially political provisions, and that experience has demonstrated that, for this reason, they are not suficiently stable to warrant their utilization as a foundation for sound economic growth under a free enterprise system. The best way—the American way—is still maximum freedom for the individual guaranteed by a wise government that provides for police protection and national defense.

History records that eventually people get the form of government they deserve. Good government, which guarantees the maximum of freedom, liberty, and development to the individual, must be based upon sound principles. We must ever remember that ideas and principles are either sound or unsound in spite of those who hold them. Freedom of achievement has produced and will continue to produce the maximum of benefits in terms of human welfare.

Freedom is an eternal principle. Heaven disapproves of force, coercion, and intimidation. Only a free people can be truly a happy people. Of all sad things in the world, the saddest is to see a people who have once known liberty and freedom and then lost it.

We are a prosperous people today because of a political-economic system founded on spiritual values, not material values alone. It is founded on freedom of choice—free agency—an eternal, God-given principle, and personal virtue.

The Founding Fathers, inspired though they were, did not invent the priceless blessing of individual freedom and respect for the dignity of man. No, that priceless gift to mankind sprang from the God of heaven and not from government. Recognizing this truth, they forged safeguards that would bind men's lust for power to the Constitution. Each new generation must learn that truth anew.

Yes, America's foundation is spiritual. Without the moral base to our system, we are no better off than other nations that are now sunk into oblivion. If we are to remain under heaven's benign protection and care, we must return to those principles which have brought us our peace, liberty, and prosperity. Our problems today are essentially problems of the spirit.

We here in America, as Theodore Roosevelt said over a half century ago, "hold in our hands the hope of the world, the fate of the coming years, and shame and disgrace will be ours if in our eyes the light of high resolve is dimmed, if we trail in the dust the golden hopes of man."

With God's help and inspiration, perhaps we may rekindle a flame of liberty that will last as long as time endures.

XI

America's Strength: The Morality of Its People

"Great nations do not fall because of external aggression; they first erode and decay inwardly. . . . The strength of a country is the sum total of the moral strength of the individuals in that country."

Our government is a system that was founded on the premise so eloquently stated by Patrick Henry, that "there is a just God who presides over the destinies of nations." In the Declaration of Independence there is an appeal to the "Supreme Judge of the World" and to "the laws of nature and nature's God."

Our system was founded on the idea that God has endowed us with rights that are inalienable, among which are life, liberty, and the pursuit of happiness. As the offspring of God, we share a common paternity that makes us literally brothers and thus gives us a common destiny. When this truth sinks into the human heart, men demand their inalienable rights. It is as the apostle Paul told the Corinthians, "Where the Spirit of the Lord is, there is liberty." (2 Corinthians 3:17.)

Ours is a system in which human rights are protected by a constitution. This is not just theory. We have bent over backwards to protect those rights; but, in some instances, our courts have given more protection to the criminal than to the law-abiding citizen.

Ours is a system based on free enterprise, which has given us the highest standard of living of any people on this earth.

Now, let us contrast our system with its alternative. Recently a remarkable speech was delivered in Washington, D.C., entitled "A Warning to America." The speaker was an exiled Russian, a Nobel Prize winner, a man who dared to speak out against the system of communism and who spent eleven years incarcerated in the Soviet prison system because he dared to oppose that system. In his speech he denounced the communist ideology as a system—

—which introduced concentration camps for the first time in the history of the world. . . .

—which was the first . . . to use false registration. Namely, they would order such and such people to come in to register. People would come in. At that point, they are taken away to be annihilated. . . .

—which introduced genocide of the peasantry. Fifteen million peasants were sent off to extermination. . . .

—which . . . artificially created a famine causing 6 million persons to die. . . .

—where for 40 years there haven't been genuine elections, but simply a farce. . . .

—without an independent judiciary, where people have no influence on external or internal policy. . . .

—where unmasked butchers of millions like Molotov . . . have never been tried in the courts, but retire on tremendous pensions. . . .

—where these farces continue today. . . .

—where the very constitution has never been carried out for one single day, where all the decisions are made somewhere high up by a small group in secret, and then released on the country like a bolt of lightning. (Alexander Solzhenitsyn, in *U.S. News and World Report,* July 14, 1975, pp. 44-50.)

Yes, today we are in a worldwide battle for the bodies and souls of men, the first of its kind between two opposing systems, between freedom and slavery, between the spirit of Christianity and the spirit of the antichrist.

Great nations do not fall because of external aggression; they first erode and decay inwardly, so that, like rotten fruit, they fall of themselves. The strength of a country is the sum total of the moral strength of the individuals in that country.

Our youth today are faced with temptations to compromise their character and standards, a bombardment of temptations the like of which has not been experienced by any other age in such intensity and sophistication. These temptations are constantly before them in literature, movies, radio, clothing fashions, television, modern music, and barracks and dormitory talk. Today Satan—who I testify is real— uses many tools to weaken and destroy character. His thrust is directed at the youth and vitality of our nation. He masquerades sex perversion as something that is natural and harmless. He uses drugs (LSD, marijuana, and others), leading magazines, underground publications, television, movies, pornographic literature, and morally destructive paperback books, filthy and obscene talk—all in an effort to see young people compromise their integrity, sacrifice their morality, and spend their moral strength for the pleasure of the moment.

God created sex, but not for self-indulgence. To quote the popular evangelist Billy Graham, "God himself implanted the physical magnetism between the sexes for two reasons: for the propagation of the human race, and for the expression of that kind of love between man and wife that makes for true oneness. His command to the first man and woman to be 'one flesh' was as important as his command to 'be fruitful and multiply.' " (As quoted by President Spencer W. Kimball, *Conference Report,* April 1974, p. 9.)

Men are not animals, left only to their instincts and self-indulgence. We are the offspring of God. God himself has set the boundaries of this sacred act. Sex outside of marriage is wrong. Every form of homosexuality is wrong. This is God's definition of chastity. Through his prophets he has declared and reiterated, "Thou shalt not commit adultery." (Exodus 20:14.)

We look back in retrospect on the war fought in Viet Nam and we mourn the loss of American life, the killed and the missing. But there are other casualties to that war we seldom mention, casualties that should cause every man who enters the military service to pause and consider their consequences.

I speak of the innocent babies born as offspring of adulterous relationships between some of our soldiers and the women of the Orient. No one knows the extent of these casualties. There are estimates of over 50,000 in Viet Nam. In Japan more than 20,000 were fathered by U.S. servicemen. Other thousands of offspring from illicit relations are in Thailand, Taiwan, and Korea. Many of these illegitimates have been abandoned by both fathers and mothers, and wander as helpless orphans, shunned by nearly all who see them. One of my colleagues has written:

> It is said that one in every ten American soldiers fathers a child by an Asian woman.
>
> Who has the right to beget illegitimate children?
>
> Who has the right to take the virtue of an Asian or any other girl, or to lose his own?
>
> Which American—at home or abroad—has the right to abandon his own flesh and blood and forget that his illegitimate child ever existed?
>
> Can the God of heaven, who holds us all accountable for our sins, overlook this wickedness?
>
> Of what good are national days of prayer if we do not support our prayers by our good works? Will God strengthen the arms of fighting men who desecrate his most holy laws? Will he prosper a nation that apparently condones these illicit practices and does little more than provide prophylactics to men who indulge?
>
> ' Are these fathers so lacking in natural affection that they are willing to completely forget and ignore their own offspring in a foreign land?
>
> We sing, almost tearfully at times, "God Bless America." But we are almost constrained to ask: "How can he?"
>
> The venereal disease rate in our war areas is frightening in the extreme. We welcome our boys home as conquering heroes, but some of them bring back a plague of venereal disease, which can destroy them.
>
> Venereal disease is a killer. It also maims, causes heart trouble, insanity, and blindness. It destroys homes, spreads corruption to innocent wives, and

blights the lives of helpless children. (Mark E. Petersen, *Conference Report*, April 1969, pp. 64-65.)

Some would justify their immorality with the argument that restrictions against it are merely religious rules, rules that are meaningless because in reality there is no God. This you will recognize is merely an untruthful rationalization designed to justify one's carnal appetite, lust, and passion. God's law is irrevocable. It applies to all, whether they believe in God or not. Everyone is subject to its penalties, no matter how one tries to rationalize or ignore them.

Immorality is next to murder in God's category of crime, and always brings with it attendant remorse. A person cannot indulge in promiscuous relations without suffering ill effects from it. He cannot do wrong and feel right—it is impossible. Anytime one breaks a law of God, he pays a penalty in heartache, in sadness, in remorse, in lack of self-respect, and he removes himself from contact with the Spirit of God. Is it any wonder that those who indulge in sex relations outside of marriage deny God?

Our nation, the United States of America, was built on the foundation of reality and spirituality. To the extent that its citizens violate God's commandments, especially his laws of morality—to that degree they weaken the country's foundation. A rejection and repudiation of God's laws could well lead our nation to its destruction just as it has to Greece and Rome. It can happen to our country unless we repent. An eminent statesman once said, "Our very civilization itself is based upon chastity, the sanctity of marriage, and the holiness of the home. Destroy these and Christian man becomes a brute." (J. Reuben Clark, Jr., *Conference Report,* October 1938, p. 137.) Home is the rock foundation, the cornerstone of civilization. No nation will be stronger than its homes and families.

God's laws are not to be trifled with. One cannot cancel out what God himself has decreed. He will not tolerate it.

We provide all young men who enter military service and who belong to The Church of Jesus Christ of Latter-day Saints with a message from our Church leaders that gives them counsel on a number of matters. May I quote from a portion of this message as it pertains to the area of chastity:

> To our young men who go into service, . . . we say live clean, keep the commandments of the Lord, pray to Him constantly to preserve you in truth and righteousness, live as you pray, and then whatever betides you the Lord will be with you and nothing will happen to you that will not be to the honor and glory of God and to your salvation and exaltation. There will come into your hearts from the living of the pure life you pray for, a joy that will pass your

powers of expression or understanding. The Lord will be always near you; He will comfort you; you will feel His presence in the hour of your greatest tribulation; He will guard and protect you to the full extent that accords with His all-wise purpose. Then, when the conflict is over and you return to your homes, having lived the righteous life, how great will be your happiness . . . that you have lived as the Lord commanded. You will return so disciplined in righteousness that thereafter all Satan's wiles and stratagems will leave you untouched. Your faith and testimony will be strong beyond breaking. You will be looked up to and revered as having passed through the fiery furnace of trial and temptation and come forth unharmed. (*Conference Report,* April 1942, p. 96.)

I think that promise is applicable to men of all faiths and beliefs.

For the happiness that will result to them, for the self-respect added to their character, for the moral strength added to our country, I urge all of our youth to be true to God and to themselves. I urge them to be chaste, to keep high moral standards, and to maintain personal integrity, honesty, and virtue.

May God bless each one of them according to their personal righteousness. May they listen and heed His counsel as He has provided it through His prophets.

XII

The American Home

"We believe marriage was ordained by God for a wise eternal purpose. The family is the basis for the righteous life. Divinely prescribed roles to father, mother, and children were given from the very beginning."

The home is the rock foundation, the cornerstone of civilization. The church, the school, and even the nation stand helpless before a weak and degraded home. No nation will rise above its homes, and no nation will long endure when the family unit is weakened or destroyed. If we accept the truth of these statements, then we must conclude that the American family has serious problems.

All is not well with this most basic institution, the American home. In fact, it is in grave danger, if not in deadly peril. There is convincing evidence that a creeping rot of moral disintegration is eating into the very vitals of this temple of American civilization. It gives cause for serious concern.

The facts are not reassuring as we soberly appraise them. Far-reaching changes, resulting from industrialization, concentration of populations, commercialization of recreation, and other activities once performed in the home, all tend to lead away from home associations.

Accompanying these changes, and in some measure resulting from them, has been a marked increase in pleasure seeking; the mad rush for money and other material things; the unwarranted indulgence of personal gratifications; the insidious inroads of tobacco, liquor, gambling, and many other tendencies in our complex modern civilization. All these have exerted a pulling power away from the home and have weakened its structure.

There seems to be a tendency for many married people to become soft and to seek a life filled with ease and the pleasure of the moment. They invite the pleasure of conjugality but often refuse to shoulder the responsibility of parenthood.

Divorce today is epidemic. The father's place at the head of the home is being challenged, and mothers have, in many instances, left the hearth to join the work force, which weakens the stability of the home. Children, growing up without strong parental guidance and spiritual influence, are allowed to roam freely. Not only does this permissiveness and lack of training sponsor indolence, but many of these youth, out of boredom, have turned to drinking, drugs, delinquency, or crime.

One great Church leader has wisely said, "No other success in life can compensate for failure in the home." (President David O. McKay.) If this nation is to endure, then the home must be safeguarded, strengthened, and restored to its rightful importance. The home is the bulwark of the nation—our most fundamental and basic institution.

Marriage, the home, and family are more than mere social institutions. They are divine, not man-made. God ordained marriage from the very beginning. In the record of that first marriage recorded in Genesis, the Lord makes four significant pronouncements: first, that it is not good for man to be alone; second, that woman was created to be a help meet for man; third, that they twain should be one flesh; and fourth, that man should leave father and mother and cleave unto his wife. (Genesis 2:18, 24.)

Later, as though to reinforce the earlier statement, the Lord said: "What therefore God hath joined together, let not man put asunder." (Matthew 19:6.) He also said, "Thou shalt love thy wife with all thy heart, and shalt cleave unto her and none else." (D&C 42:22.)

This first marriage, instituted by God, was between two immortal beings. Marriage was thus intended to be eternal. Following the consummation of this marriage, God gave Adam and Eve important instruction about the perpetuation of the family, instruction that has never been rescinded: "Be fruitful, and multiply, and replenish the earth." (Genesis 1:28.)

The scriptures teach that man was created in the image and likeness of his Creator. (Genesis 1:26-27.) Fundamental to the theology of The Church of Jesus Christ of Latter-day Saints is the belief that the purpose of man's whole existence is to grow into the likeness and image of God. We accept quite literally the Savior's mandate: "Be ye therefore perfect, even as your Father which is in heaven is perfect." (Matthew 5:48.)

We believe God to be the personal Heavenly Father to all mankind, that all mortal beings are literally His spirit offspring. We worship God as a personal, all-knowing, all-powerful being, endowed with all the attributes of perfection. As God's literal offspring, we believe man to be His only creation blessed with His image and His

likeness. Our children sing a song from the time they learn to talk
that impresses upon them their celestial as well as mortal heritage:

> "I am a child of God,
> And he has sent me here,
> Has given me an earthly home
> With parents kind and dear.
>
> "I am a child of God,
> And so my needs are great;
> Help me to understand his words
> Before it grows too late.
>
> "I am a child of God,
> Rich blessings are in store;
> If I but learn to do his will,
> I'll live with him once more.
>
> "Lead me, guide me, walk beside me,
> Help me find the way.
> Teach me all that I must do
> To live with him someday."
> —*Sing with Me*, no. B-76

Yes, we believe marriage was ordained by God for a wise eternal
purpose. The family is the basis for the righteous life. Divinely prescribed roles to father, mother, and children were given from the very
beginning. God established that fathers were to preside in the home.
Fathers are to procreate, provide, love, teach, and direct. A mother's
role is also God-ordained. Mothers are to conceive, bear, nourish,
love, and train. They are the helpmates and counselors to their hus-
bands.

Children are likewise counseled in holy writ in their duty to
parents. Paul the apostle wrote: "Children, obey your parents in the
Lord: for this is right. Honour thy father and mother; (which is the
first commandment with promise;) that it may be well with thee, and
thou mayest live long on the earth." (Ephesians 6:1-3.) When
parents, in companionship, love, and unity, fulfill their heaven-
imposed responsibility, and children respond with love and obedience,
great joy is the result.

Did the God of heaven who created and intended marriage and
family to be the source of man's greatest joy, his dearest possession
while on this earth, intend that it end at death? Do marriage and
families pertain only to this transitory state? Are all our sympathies,

affections, and love for each other a thing of naught, to be cast off in death? Another distinctive teaching of Latter-day Saint theology is our belief in revelation from God to latter-day prophets. We testify that Joseph Smith was a prophet raised up by God to restore many great truths that had been lost because of the absence of revelation. Through him, God revealed the eternity of the marriage covenant and the timelessness of the family. The effect that this teaching has upon Church members is most pronounced. One of the early apostles in the Church recorded his feelings about this doctrine in these words:

> I received from [Joseph Smith] the first idea of eternal family organization, and the eternal union of the sexes in those inexpressibly endearing relationships which none but the highly intellectual, the refined and pure in heart, know how to prize, and which are at the very foundation of everything worthy to be called happiness.
>
> Till then I had learned to esteem kindred affections and sympathies as appertaining solely to this transitory state, as something from which the heart must be entirely weaned, in order to be fitted for its heavenly state.
>
> It was Joseph Smith who taught me how to prize the endearing relationships of father and mother, husband and wife; of brother and sister, son and daughter.
>
> It was from him that I learned that the wife of my bosom might be secured to me for time and all eternity; and that the refined sympathies and affections which endeared us to each other emanated from the foundation of divine eternal love. It was from him that I learned that we might cultivate these affections, and grow and increase in the same to all eternity.
>
> It was from him that I learned the true dignity and destiny of a son of God, clothed with an eternal priesthood, as the patriarch and sovereign of his [family]. It was from him that I learned that the highest dignity of womanhood was, to stand as a queen and priestess with her husband. . . .
>
> I had loved before, but I knew not why. But now I loved—with a pureness—an intensity of elevated, exalted feeling, which would lift my soul from the transitory things of this grovelling sphere and expand it as the ocean. I felt that God was my heavenly Father indeed; that Jesus was my brother, and that the wife of my bosom was an immortal, eternal companion; a kind ministering angel, given to me as a comfort, and a crown of glory for ever and ever. In short, I could now love with the spirit and with the understanding also. (*Autobiography of Parley P. Pratt*, Deseret Book Co., 1975, pp. 297-98.)

Because of this confidence in the perpetuity of the home and family into the eternities, we build our most elaborate and expensive structures—temples of God, so that man, woman, and their children may be bound together by covenant in an everlasting union that will transcend all the limitations of this mortal sphere. It is because of this belief that the Church decries divorce, and that we are actively engaged in teaching fathers that their most important duty is within the walls of their own homes, and mothers, that they should be full-time mothers in the home. It is why we encourage parents to teach their children fundamental spiritual principles that will instill faith in God, faith in the family, and faith in their country. There is no other institution that can take the place of the family, nor fulfill its essential function.

Yes, families are intended to have joy. President David O. McKay once said, "In the well-ordered home we may experience on earth a taste of heaven." (*Conference Report,* April 1969, p. 5.) How true that is!

My plea to all who read these words is that we strengthen our families so that our memories of home may be happy ones, that our home life may be a foretaste of heaven.

God intended the family to be eternal. With all my soul, I testify to the truth of that declaration. May He bless us to strengthen our homes and the lives of each family member so that in due time we can report to our Heavenly Father in His celestial home that we are all there—father, mother, sister, brother, all who hold each other dear. In this, the greatest of all nations, in this land choice above all others, I pay humble tribute to the home. It is America's greatest strength.

God grant that the love and unity in all our homes will be preserved to transcend the bounds of this mortal life.

XIII

Meeting the Challenge

"If we as a nation are to long remain under heaven's benign protection and care, we should return to those principles that have brought us peace, liberty, and prosperity."

This nation is distinctive among the nations of mankind. It is not just one among the families of nations, but it has a unique origin, purpose, and destiny. The foundation of this nation is spiritual. It was founded on belief in the sovereignty of God and that he—not government—granted man his rights. Furthermore, the Founding Fathers gave deliberate acknowledgment that the hand of God was in the events that brought about our independence. Here are a few of their testimonies:

George Washington: "The success, which has hitherto attended our united efforts, we owe to the gracious interposition of Heaven, and to that interposition let us gratefully ascribe the praise of victory, and the blessings of peace." (To the Executive of New Hampshire, November 3, 1789.)

Alexander Hamilton: "The Sacred Rights of mankind are not to be rummaged from among old parchments or musty records. They are written . . . by the Hand of Divinity itself." ("The Farmer Refuted," 1775.)

Thomas Jefferson: "The God who gave us life, gave us liberty at the same time." (Rights of British America, 1774.)

John Quincy Adams: "From the day of the Declaration . . . [the American people] were bound by the laws of God . . . and by the laws of the Gospel, which they nearly all acknowledged as the rules of their conduct." (Oration celebrating July 4, 1821.)

It was not just incidental nor was it mere political platitude that the name of God was mentioned in the Declaration of Independence four times, and that our adopted national motto became "In God We Trust." From the life of our illustrious founder, George Washington, we have an example of rectitude worthy of emulation by all public servants, an example that demonstrates a consistency between his private morality and public behavior. In light of past and present indiscretions by public officials, it would seem that this is a lesson that needs to be relearned.

It is evident from the vantage point of two hundred years that this country today enjoys an unparalleled freedom and prosperity. The facts speak for themselves.

Few nations possess the freedoms we do: freedom to speak, freedom to own property and business, freedom to worship, freedom to print, freedom to travel at home and abroad, freedom to censure even public officials, and freedom of private enterprise. No other country has been more richly blessed or more generous in terms of money and food.

Of whose who malign our country or system, we ask, by what source did we receive such blessings and prosperity?

The source of all these blessings is God, because to a great extent we have been a God-fearing, Christ-worshiping people. Yet it should be evident to all who survey the social, political, and domestic landscape before us today, that we have departed from the ways of our forefathers and the path they marked out for us. In recent years we have witnessed a corrosion of the constitutional government established by our forebears, and a departure from the laws of God. No longer may it be said that we have a nation united *under* God. In Abraham Lincoln's words, "We have forgotten God."

There are some in this land, among whom I count myself, whose faith it is that America is "a land choice above all other lands" to the Lord, and that we shall remain on this land only as we remain in God's divine favor.

There are principles that may bring us back into heaven's favor again. These principles are embodied in the Decalogue, or the Ten Commandments. They came from God Himself to Moses, and form the foundation of civilized society. Designed by the Almighty, these laws plumb the depths of human motives and urges, and, if adhered to, will regulate the baser passions of mankind. No nation has ever perished that has kept the commandments of God.

Neither permanent government nor civilization will long endure that violates these laws. The conscience of all right-thinking people declares this to be so. "America cannot remain strong by ignoring the commandments of the Lord." (President Spencer W. Kimball, June 3, 1976.)

Again, our vantage point today, two hundred years after the birth of this favored nation, yields to us a foresight to see that if we as a nation are to long remain under heaven's benign protection and care, we should return to those principles that have brought us peace, liberty, and prosperity. Our problems today are essentially problems of the spirit. The solution is not more wealth, more food, more technology, more government, or instruments of destruction. The solution is personal and national reformation. In short, it is to bring our national character ahead of our technological and material advances. Repentance is the sovereign remedy to our problems.

This nation is God-ordained for a glorious purpose. It is an ensign of liberty to all other nations. This liberty will be maintained as we keep the commandments of God. Righteousness is the indispensable ingredient to liberty.

Our Future Destiny

*"America is a great
and glorious nation with
a divine mission,
brought into being under the
inspiration of heaven.
It is truly a land choice above
all others."*

XIV

A Message
to the World

"To rulers and peoples of all nations, we solemnly declare again that the God of heaven has established His latter-day kingdom upon the earth in fulfillment of prophecies."

Our Lord and Savior Jesus Christ, after restoring his gospel in our day and establishing his church, even The Church of Jesus Christ of Latter-day Saints, revealed through the Prophet Joseph Smith the following:

"Hearken, O ye people of my church, saith the voice of him who dwells on high, and whose eyes are upon all men; yea, verily I say: Hearken ye people from afar; and ye that are upon the islands of the sea, listen together.

"For verily the voice of the Lord is unto all men, and there is none to escape; . . .

"And the voice of warning shall be unto all people, by the mouths of my disciples, whom I have chosen in these last days." (D&C 1:1-2, 4.)

Toward the end of his mortal ministry, the Lord commanded the Prophet, "Make a solemn proclamation of my gospel . . . to all the kings of the world, to the four corners thereof . . . and to all the nations of the earth." He was to invite them to "come to the light of truth" and use their means to build up the kingdom of God on earth. (See D&C 124:2-12.)

In the spirit of this divine direction, on the sixth day of April in 1845, less than a year after the Prophet Joseph Smith and his brother Hyrum had mingled their blood with that of the other martyrs of true religion, the Council of the Twelve made such a proclamation. They addressed it:

> To all the Kings of the World;
> To the President of the United States of America;
> To the Governors of the several States;
> And to the Rulers and People of all Nations:
> Know ye:
> That the kingdom of God has come: as has been predicted by ancient prophets, and prayed for in all ages; even that kingdom which shall fill the whole earth, and shall stand for ever.

The great Eloheem . . . has been pleased once more to speak from the heavens: and also to commune with man upon the earth, by means of open visions, and by the ministration of Holy Messengers.

By this means the great and eternal High Priesthood, after the Order of His Son, even the Apostleship, has been restored; or, returned to the earth.

This High Priesthood, or Apostleship, holds the keys of the kingdom of God, and power to bind on earth that which shall be bound in heaven; and to loose on earth that which shall be loosed in heaven. And, in fine, to do, and to administer in all things pertaining to the ordinances, organization, government and direction of the kingdom of God.

Being established in these last days for the restoration of all things spoken by the prophets since the world began; and in order to prepare the way for the coming of the Son of Man.

And we now bear witness that his coming is near at hand; and not many years hence, the nations and their kings shall see him coming in the clouds of heaven with power and great glory.

In order to meet this great event there must needs be a preparation.

Therefore we send unto you with authority from on high, and command you all to repent and humble yourselves as little children before the majesty of the Holy One; and come unto Jesus [Christ] with a broken heart and a contrite spirit, and be baptized in his name for the remission of sins (that is, be buried in the water in the likeness of his burial and rise again to newness of life, in the likeness of his resurrection), and you shall receive the gift of the Holy Spirit, through the laying on of the hands of the Apostles and elders, of this great and last dispensation of mercy to man.

This Spirit shall bear witness to you, of the truth of our testimony; and shall enlighten your minds, and be in you as the spirit of prophecy and revelation. It shall bring things past to your understanding and remembrance; and shall show you things to come. . . .

By the light of this Spirit, received through the ministration of the ordinances—by the power and authority of the Holy Apostleship and Priesthood, you will be enabled to understand, and to be the children of light; and thus be prepared to escape all the things that are coming on the earth, and so stand before the Son of Man.

We testify that the foregoing doctrine is the doctrine or gospel of Jesus Christ, in its fulness; and that it is the only true, everlasting, and unchangeable gospel; and the only plan revealed on earth whereby man can be saved. (*Messages of the First Presidency*. Bookcraft, 1965, 1:252-66.)

It seems fitting and proper to me that we should reaffirm the great truths pronounced in this declaration, and that we should proclaim them anew to the world.

To the rulers and peoples of all nations, we solemnly declare again that the God of heaven has established His latter-day kingdom upon the earth in fulfillment of prophecies. Holy angels have again communed with men on the earth. God has again revealed Himself from the heavens and restored to the earth His holy priesthood with power to administer in all the sacred ordinances necessary for the exaltation of His children. His church has been reestablished among men with all the spiritual gifts enjoyed anciently. All this is done in preparation for Christ's second coming. The great and dreadful day of the Lord is near at hand. In preparation for this great event and as a means of escaping the impending judgments, inspired messengers have gone, and are going, forth to the nations of the earth carrying this testimony and warning.

The nations of the earth continue in their sinful and unrighteous ways. Much of the unbounded knowledge with which men have been blessed has been used to destroy mankind instead of to bless the children of men as the Lord intended. Two great world wars, with fruitless efforts at lasting peace, are solemn evidence that peace has been taken from the earth because of the wickedness of the people. Nations cannot endure in sin. They will be broken up but the kingdom of God will endure forever.

Therefore, as humble servants of the Lord, we call upon the leaders of nations to humble themselves before God, to seek His inspiration and guidance. We call upon rulers and people alike to repent of their evil ways. Turn unto the Lord, seek His forgiveness, and unite yourselves in humility with His kingdom. There is no other way. If you will do this, your sins will be blotted out, peace will come and remain, and you will become a part of the kingdom of God in preparation for Christ's second coming. But if you refuse to repent, to accept the testimony of His inspired messengers, or to unite yourselves with God's kingdom, then the terrible judgments and calamities promised the wicked will be yours.

The Lord in His mercy has provided a way of escape. The voice of warning is unto all people by the mouths of His servants. If this voice is not heeded, the angels of destruction will increasingly go forth, and the chastening hand of Almighty God will be felt upon the nations, as decreed, until a full end thereof will be the result. Wars, devastation, and untold suffering will be your lot except you turn unto the Lord in humble repentance. Destruction, even more terrible and far-reaching than attended the last great war, will come with certainty unless rulers and people alike repent and cease their evil and godless ways. God will not be mocked. He will not permit the sins of sexual immorality, secret murderous combinations, the killing of the unborn, and disregard for all His holy commandments and the messages of His servants to go unheeded without grievous punishment for such wickedness. The nations of the world cannot endure in sin. The way of escape is clear. The immutable laws of God remain steadfastly in the heavens above. When men and nations refuse to abide by them, the penalty must follow. They will be wasted away. Sin demands punishment.

When the voice of warning goes forth it is always attended by testimony. In the great declaration issued by the apostles of the Lord Jesus Christ in 1845, this is the testimony which was borne, and we who are the apostles today renew it as our witness:

> We say, then, in life or in death, in bonds or free, that the great God has spoken in this age.—*And we know it.*
>
> He has given us the Holy Priesthood and the Apostleship, and the keys of the kingdom of God, to bring about the restoration of all things as promised by the holy prophets of old.—*And we know it.*
>
> He has revealed the origin and the Records of the aboriginal tribes of America, and their future destiny.—*And we know it.*
>
> He has revealed the fulness of the gospel, with its gifts, blessings, and ordinances.—*And we know it.*
>
> He has commanded *us* to bear witness of it, first to the Gentiles, and then to the remnants of Israel and the Jews.—*And we know it.*
>
> He has said that, if they do not repent, and come to the knowledge of the truth, . . . and also put away all murder, lying, pride, priestcraft, whoredom, and secret abomination, they shall soon perish from the earth, and be cast down to hell.—*And we know it.*
>
> He has said that when . . . the gospel in all its fulness is preached to all nations for a witness and testimony, he will come, and all Saints with him, to reign on the earth one thousand years.—*And we know it.*
>
> He has said that he will not come in his glory and destroy the wicked till these warnings were given and these preparations were made for his reception.—*And we know it.*
>
> Heaven and earth shall pass away, but not one jot or tittle of his revealed word shall fail to be fulfilled.
>
> Therefore, again we say to all people, Repent, and be baptized in the name of Jesus Christ, for remission of sins; and you shall receive the Holy Spirit, and shall know the truth, and be numbered with the house of Israel. (*Messages of the First Presidency* 1:263-64.)

I know that God lives, that He is a personal being, the Father of our spirits, and that He loves His children and hears and answers their righteous prayers. I know that it is His will that His children be happy. It is His desire to bless us all. I know that Jesus Christ is the Son of God, our Elder Brother, the very Creator and Redeemer of the world. I know that God has again established His kingdom on the earth in fulfillment of prophecy and that it will never be overcome, but it shall ultimately hold universal dominion in the earth and Jesus Christ shall reign as its King forever.

I know that God in His goodness has again revealed Himself from the heavens and that Joseph Smith was called of God to reestablish that kingdom—The Church of Jesus Christ of Latter-day Saints. I testify that He accomplished this work, that He laid the foundations, and that He committed to the Church the keys and powers to continue the great latter-day work, which He began under the direction of Almighty God.

I know that Joseph Smith, although slain as a martyr to the truth, still lives, and that, as head of his dispensation—the greatest of all gospel dispensations—he will continue so to stand throughout the eternities to come. He is a prophet of God, a seer and a revelator, as are his successors. I know that the inspiration of the Lord is directing the Church today because I have felt of its power. I know that the First Presidency and other General Authorities of the Church have as their object and purpose the glory of God and the exaltation of His children. And finally, I know that no person who does not receive this work can be saved in the celestial kingdom of God and escape the condemnation of the Judge of us all.

XV

The Mormons and Our Message

"Our message to the world is that the kingdom of which Daniel prophesied is now on the earth. . . . As Jesus said to men of His day, so we say to men of today: 'The kingdom of God is in the midst of you.' "

I n the Old Testament it is written that in the last days "the God of heaven [shall] set up a kingdom." (Daniel 2:44.) Daniel likened the early beginnings of this kingdom to "a stone . . . cut out without hands," which would become "a great mountain" to fill the whole earth. (See Daniel 2:34-35.)

Our message to the world is that the kingdom of which Daniel prophesied is now on the earth. Its early beginnings were as inconspicuous as a small stone rolling down a mountain. Today, partly because of its accelerated growth, The Church of Jesus Christ of Latter-day Saints is no longer ignored. Prejudice has largely subsided as people have come in contact with Mormons and their message.

We realize that our message is impressive as well as startling to some. It provokes the sincere inquiry, "Did not Jesus establish the kingdom of God, His church, in His own time? Why do you claim that the kingdom of God is only a latter-day event?" This sincere inquiry is deserving of an answer.

Jesus did establish His church on this earth in His time, which He declared was "the kingdom of God has already come unto you." (Luke 17:21, Inspired Version.) His church had an authorized ministry personally ordained by the Savior Himself. To a selected number, whom He designated as apostles, He bestowed the "keys of the kingdom." These keys, or rights, authorized the apostles to be legal administrators of the gospel of our Lord and the ordinances that pertained thereto. These keys further enabled the apostles to bind ordinances for time as well as eternity. Referring to this power, Jesus said to His apostles, "Whatsoever ye shall bind on earth shall be bound in heaven: and whatsoever ye shall loose on earth shall be loosed in heaven." (Matthew 18:18.)

After our Lord's literal physical resurrection, but before His ascension into heaven, He commanded the apostles to "teach all nations" His gospel. (See Matthew 28:19.) He further exhorted them to be "witnesses . . . in Jerusalem, and in all Judea, and in Samaria, and unto the uttermost part of the earth." (Acts 1:8.) Obedient to that command, the apostles took the gospel throughout the world. The gospel message, once confined to Palestine, became a worldwide message. From its centers in Jerusalem, and later Antioch of Syria, Christianity spread to foreign frontiers with a harvest of converts. As expressed by Jesus in the parable, the mustard seed became as a tree with its branches extending into various parts of the earth. Because of its rapid growth, the church became noticeable. Persecutions followed, first by the Jews and then by the Roman government. Some of the leaders of the church were martyred, including James, Peter, and Paul. Disaffection spread among the members in the infant church. Since valiance to the cause meant certain death, some chose apostasy. Eventually, the apostles were killed, leaving no legal administrators on the earth to regulate the affairs of the kingdom, to settle doctrinal disputes, or to pass on the authority they held.

With the passing of the apostles and the loss of the priesthood keys, corrupt doctrines were introduced into the church. In the words of one eminent historian, "Christianity did not destroy paganism; it adopted it. The Greek mind, dying, came to a transmigrated [new] life in the theology and liturgy of the Church." (Will Durant, *The Story of Civilization*, New York: Simon and Schuster, 1944, 3:595.)

By the second and third centuries, widespread changes had been made in the pure doctrines and ordinances given by the Savior. The church that Jesus had established and sanctioned was no longer on this earth.

But had this general apostasy not been forseen? Speaking of His kingdom, Jesus said on two occasions, ". . . the kingdom of heaven suffereth violence, and the violent take it by force" (Matthew 11:12), and "The kingdom of God shall be taken from you [the Jews], and given to a nation [the Gentiles] bringing forth the fruits thereof" (Matthew 21:43).

This was not the same kingdom about which Daniel prophesied, for he said that the kingdom of the last days would never be destroyed or "be left to other people." (Daniel 2:44.) Jesus said that the kingdom established in His time would be "given to a nation bringing forth the fruits thereof." In other words, Jesus knew, as did the apostles, that an apostasy would take place before His kingdom would be finally established as a prelude to and preparation for His second coming.

The apostle Paul wrote to members of the church at Thessalonica that the second coming of Jesus Christ "shall not come, except there come a falling away first." (2 Thessalonians 2:3.) And Peter likewise wrote: "There shall be false teachers among you, who privily shall bring in damnable heresies . . . and many shall follow their pernicious ways." (2 Peter 2:1-2.)

So the world entered that long night of apostasy, the Dark Ages. The church, no longer sanctioned by God, exercised an oppressive tyranny on the minds of men and shackled them with chains of false traditions. Truth was turned to superstition, joy to despair, and worship to ritual. Before the gospel could again shine forth its resplendent light, religious and political freedom first had to be restored. God determined that it take place in America.

This land had been preserved as a continent apart from the religious oppression, tyranny, and intolerance of Europe. In time, emigrants came to the new land and established colonies. By and large, they were a God-fearing people. A war was fought for their independence, and by God's intervention, victory was achieved. By that same omnipotent power the Constitution was born, which guaranteed religious and political liberty. Only then was the time propitious for the kingdom of God—that "stone . . . cut out without hands"—to be restored.

A prophet of God was sent to this new nation. This occurred in the year 1805, only sixteen years after the ratification of the Constitution. The prophet's name was Joseph Smith.

In his fifteenth year, while troubled because of the "tumult of opinions" about which church was right, this young man sought an answer in prayer. Secluding himself in a grove of trees near his father's farm in Palmyra, New York, he asked of God. His prayer was answered with a glorious manifestation in which he saw God the Father, and His Son, Jesus Christ. These are his words:

"I saw a pillar of light exactly over my head, above the brightness of the sun. . . . When the light rested upon me I saw two Personages, whose brightness and glory defy all description, standing above me in the air. One of them spake unto me, calling me by name and said, . . . *This is my Beloved Son. Hear Him!*" (Joseph Smith 2:17.)

He was commanded to join none of the churches of his day. In time, other heavenly messengers came to this earth and conferred on him those keys or rights to administer the affairs of the kingdom of God. With the restoration of the keys, the gospel of Jesus Christ and ordinances of salvation became available to mankind.

This is the glorious message we desire to share with the world, that through God the Father and His Son, Jesus Christ, the kingdom of God has been restored. It is the greatest message since the resurrection of Jesus Christ. Like the stone that Daniel saw, the kingdom is now rolling forward in the earth to fulfill its destiny to fill the whole earth.

We are under divine commandment to see that this is done. In a revelation given to the Prophet Joseph Smith in October 1831, the Lord proclaimed: "The keys of the kingdom of God are committed unto man on the earth, and from thence shall the gospel roll forth unto the ends of the earth, as the stone which is cut out of the mountain without hands shall roll forth, until it has filled the whole earth.

"Call upon the Lord, that his kingdom may go forth upon the earth, that the inhabitants thereof may receive it, and be prepared for the days to come, in the which the Son of Man shall come down in heaven, clothed in the brightness of his glory, to meet the kingdom of God which is set up on the earth." (D&C 65:2, 5.)

"Wherefore, may the kingdom of God go forth, that the kingdom of heaven may come. . . ." (D&C 65:6.) As Jesus said to men of His day, so we say to men of today: "The kingdom of God is in the midst of you."

XVI

A Message to the Lamanites

The three prominent precepts in the Book of Mormon are: (1) that Jesus is the promised Messiah, our Lord and Redeemer; (2) that this land is a land choice above all other lands; and (3) that God has preserved a promised people because of special covenants they or their progenitors willfully made with God.

Mormons have an Article of Faith that reads: "We believe the Bible to be the word of God as far as it is translated correctly; we also believe the Book of Mormon to be the word of God."

Briefly, here is an account of the origin of this book.

On a spring day in the year 1820 in the state of New York, a young boy named Joseph Smith went into a grove of trees on his father's farm to pray. He sought guidance. He wanted to join a church, but he was confused as to which one. While seeking an answer, he read one day these words from the Bible: "If any of you lack wisdom, let him ask of God, that giveth to all men liberally, and upbraideth not; and it shall be given him." (James 1:5.) This Joseph did. In response to his prayer, our Heavenly Father and His Son, Jesus Christ, appeared to him. Joseph was told to join none of the churches.

Joseph was to learn that Christ established His church in former days when He was here on earth. Being the Church of Jesus Christ, it was vitalized by revelation from heaven. Doctrinal disputes were settled on the basis of revelation. But persecution against the church and disaffection from within caused the apostles and prophets to be taken from the earth. This removed the appointed servants who were to receive revelation for the church at large, to keep its membership in a unity of doctrine and faith. So revelation ceased and scripture ended. New doctrines and creeds of uninspired men were introduced into the church. As predicted in the scriptures, there was an apostasy.

But it was also predicted in the scripture that the Lord would restore His church in these latter days prior to His second coming. Like the former-day church, His restored church was to have apostles, prophets, and current revelation, which added new scripture. We declare that this prophecy has come to pass. Through the Prophet Joseph Smith the Lord has established His church again on earth. Within it are found apostles and prophets, revelation, and new scripture. One portion of the new scripture coming forth in our modern day is the Book of Mormon.

On the evening of September 21, 1823, an angel named Moroni appeared to the Prophet Joseph Smith. Moroni was the last of a long line of ancient prophets from a mighty civilization that once inhabited the American continent centuries ago. The angel told Joseph Smith that the history of these early inhabitants of America was written on metallic plates that lay buried in a nearby hill.

These records covered a period of American history from the time of the Tower of Babel until about 421 A.D. The engraved records were handed down from generation to generation and were abridged by a prophet named Mormon. Mormon's son Moroni added some additional writings and then laid the records in the earth, where they remained until he delivered them to Joseph Smith. By the inspiration of God, Joseph Smith translated these records and titled the record after its author. That is why this record is called the Book of Mormon.

There were other witnesses besides Joseph Smith who saw the angel and the plates. Their written testimony is found printed in the front of each copy of the Book of Mormon.

The Bible is a scriptural account of God's dealings with His children in the Old World. The Book of Mormon is a scriptural account of God's dealings with His children in the Americas.

Of this sacred volume of scripture, the Prophet Joseph Smith said, ". . . the Book of Mormon was the most correct of any book on earth, and the keystone of our religion, and a man would get nearer to God by abiding by its precepts, than by any other book." (*Teachings of the Prophet Joseph Smith,* p. 194.)

I emphasize three of the prominent precepts in this book: a promised Lord, a promised land, and a promised people.

The first and most central theme of the Book of Mormon is that Jesus is the promised Messiah, our Lord and Redeemer. He came to redeem mankind from a lost and fallen condition brought about by Adam's transgression. Nearly all Christian churches accepted this truth as fundamental to their faith when the Book of Mormon was published to the world in 1830. The fact that another book had come forth as a second witness to Christ's divinity was regarded by many churches as being both superfluous and spurious. They said, "We already have a Bible. Why do we need another?"

But the nineteenth century was not the twentieth. Who but God and inspired prophets could have foreseen the need for an additional witness for the divinity of His Son? Who but God and inspired prophets could have foreseen the time when self-evident truths in the Bible were made obscure by virtue of modern translations—translations made by scholars who seriously challenged the divinity of Jesus Christ as the Son of God? Who but God and inspired prophets could have foreseen the day when ministers of prominent denominations would openly challenge the divinity of Jesus Christ? One doctor of divinity, in lecturing to a large group of students in the last decade, said: "Who knows but what in the year 2004 or some other year, there will live a man who will live more perfectly than did Jesus. Then we will worship him as the Son of God, rather than Jesus. The reason we worship Jesus as the Son of God is because he lived the most perfect life of any man of whom we have knowledge."

Others of the clergy have challenged the virgin birth account in the New Testament as a myth. The literal resurrection of the Master is regarded by some as a hoax perpetrated upon a gullible community by Jesus' apostles.

I received some time ago a letter from a long-time friend, a lay worker in his own church. He closed his letter with the words, "God bless you and your wonderful work. I pray that Satan be kept out of your church—since we have failed to keep him out of ours!"

Concluding a three-day convention, attended by 3500 people from forty states and five foreign countries, this occurred. An informal, unprogrammed banquet was held. After the dinner, the chairman announced he would call on four or five men from the audience to come to the podium and speak from their hearts about anything they would like to say. The first called was from the South—a publisher of farm magazines. This is the substance of his remarks: "Ladies and gentlemen, I've been accused of leaving my church, but I say to you, I didn't leave my church—my church left me. My church no longer teaches that God lives, that He is a personal God who hears and answers prayers as I was taught as a child in my Sunday School classes and at my mother's knee. My church no longer teaches the basic concepts of Christianity—the reality of the holy atonement, the resurrection, the final judgment. My church no longer teaches these basic truths. I say to you, I still believe them. The pulpit of my church has become a pipeline to collectivism—teaching the social gospel, but denying the basic concepts of Christianity. I didn't leave my church, my church left me."

Yes, only an omniscient God and prophets whom He inspired

could have foreseen this age of unbelief and the need for an additional witness to Christ for our modern age.

How does the Book of Mormon provide a second witness of the mission of Jesus Christ to the Bible? Book of Mormon prophets testified hundreds of years before the birth of Jesus that He would be born of a virgin named Mary and that His name would be Jesus Christ. Long before Jesus was born these prophets outlined His public ministry and declared that He would work mighty miracles, such as "healing the sick, raising the dead, causing the lame to walk, the blind to receive their sight, and the deaf to hear, and curing all manner of diseases." (Mosiah 3:5.)

Though He was God, and that by virtue of the fact that God our Heavenly Father was His literal Father, the Book of Mormon testifies that He was susceptible to mortal infirmities: temptation, pain, hunger, thirst, and fatigue.

The Book of Mormon tells of the Messiah's great atoning sacrifice. It describes how Jesus willingly suffered the pains of all men and specifies the conditions by which His atonement may bring us to a remission of our sins, a peace of conscience, and great joy.

Many years before His first coming, Book of Mormon prophets foretold that He would be rejected by His nation, the Jews; that He would be scourged, crucified, and buried. But these same prophets also foretold that He would arise again from the dead, and because of His resurrection, all mankind will be resurrected—every mortal creature. These prophets testified that eventually Jesus will come again to judge the world.

The Book of Mormon is a second witness to Jesus Christ because it tells the account of His ministry to the people on this continent following His ascension in Jerusalem. Permit me to share with you the beautiful account of His glorious appearance to these people:

> [The people of Nephi] cast their eyes up again towards heaven; and behold, they saw a Man descending out of heaven; and he was clothed in a white robe; and he came down and stood in the midst of them; and the eyes of the whole multitude were turned upon him, and they durst not open their mouths, even one to another, and wist not what it meant, for they thought it was an angel that had appeared unto them.
>
> And it came to pass that he stretched forth his hand and spake unto the people, saying:
>
> Behold, I am Jesus Christ, whom the prophets testified shall come into the world.
>
> And behold, I am the light and life of the world; and I have drunk out of that bitter cup which the Father hath given me, and have glorified the Father in taking upon me the sins of the world, in the which I have suffered the will of the Father in all things from the beginning.

And it came to pass that when Jesus had spoken these words the whole multitude fell to the earth; for they remembered that it had been prophesied among them that Christ should show himself unto them after his ascension into heaven.

And it came to pass that the Lord spake unto them saying:

Arise and come forth unto me, that ye may thrust your hands into my side, and also that ye may feel the prints of the nails in my hands and in my feet, that ye may know that I am the God of Israel, and the God of the whole earth, and have been slain for the sins of the world.

And it came to pass that the multitude went forth, and thrust their hands into his side, and did feel the prints of the nails in his hands and in his feet; and this they did do, going forth one by one until they had all gone forth, and did see with their eyes and did feel with their hands, and did know of a surety and did bear record, that it was he, of whom it was written by the prophets, that should come. (3 Nephi 11:8-15.)

The Book of Mormon is a second witness to Jesus Christ because it contains the plain and precious truths of His gospel. Within this sacred record is the fullness of the gospel of Jesus Christ; in other words, the Lord's requirements for salvation. Here are the Savior's words: "And whoso believeth in me, and is baptized, the same shall be saved; and they are they who shall inherit the kingdom of God. And whoso believeth not in me, and is not baptized, shall be damned. . . . Ye must repent, and be baptized in my name, and become as a little child, or ye can in nowise inherit the kingdom of God. . . . verily, I say unto you, . . . this is my doctrine." (3 Nephi 11:33-34, 38-39.)

Perhaps you have questions such as these: What is the purpose of baptism? What is the correct mode of baptism? Who has the authority to baptize? How does one become a member of the Church of Jesus Christ? By what name is the Church of Jesus Christ to be called? How does one obtain a forgiveness of his sins? What is the state of the soul between death and the resurrection? Will I live again? What is the state of a resurrected being? How can I receive a fullness of joy?

Within the pages of the Book of Mormon are answers to these questions. It is for this reason that an angel of God told Joseph Smith that "the fulness of the everlasting gospel was contained in it." (Joseph Smith 2:34.) Now perhaps you can understand why Joseph Smith said that "a man would get nearer to God by abiding by its precepts, than by any other book."

The question is sometimes asked, Are Mormons Christians? We declare the divinity of Jesus Christ. We look to Him as the only source of our salvation. We strive to live His teachings, and we look forward to the time when He shall come again on this earth to rule and reign as King of kings and Lord of lords. In the words of a Book of Mormon prophet, we say to men today, "There shall be no other name given nor any other way nor means whereby salvation can come unto the children of men, only in and through the name of Christ, the Lord Omnipotent." (Mosiah 3:17.)

A second theme emphasized in the Book of Mormon is that the land we live upon, this land of North and South America, is a land choice above all other lands.

One thing becomes apparent as we study the scriptures. That is, God has had a hand in the history of mankind. His purpose is to bring to pass the immortality of all of His children and the eternal life to those of His children who willingly comply with His commandments. You will notice that I have made a distinction between the terms *immortality* and *eternal life*. Immortality is a free gift to all men because of the resurrection of Jesus Christ. Eternal life is the quality of life enjoyed by our Heavenly Father. Those who fully comply with His commandments receive the promise that they will have this quality of life. "He that believeth on the Son hath everlasting [eternal] life: and he that believeth not the Son shall not see life." (John 3:36.) The great purpose of God throughout the history of mankind has been to bring His children to eternal life. It is a purpose motivated out of the infinite love that He has for all of us, His children.

Because of His infinite love, God has seen fit from the very beginning of this earth to give men commandments. These commandments were designed to exalt man from His fallen state to a state of righteousness and joy. They were also designed to bring about domestic accord in homes, communities, and nations. History has shown that when individuals and nations have kept the commandments of God they have been happy, prosperous, and most blessed; when they have departed from those commandments, pride, strife, contention, and warfare have resulted. There have been times in the history of mankind when nations have brought down upon themselves the judgments of God, and this because they deliberately chose a course contrary to God's purposes and their own happiness. Famine, disease, and war—that terrifying triad of human tragedy— have led many great civilizations to ruin and oblivion. The history of mankind is a testament of this fact.

Every American citizen should understand God's purpose for this great nation in which we live, and how we may avert the decadence and destruction suffered by other mighty empires. Here is what the Book of Mormon says about the founding of this nation and how we may survive as a free country.

1. All nations that inhabit this land are bound by an everlasting decree from God, a decree that the inhabitants of this land shall serve God or they shall be swept off. (See Ether 2:10.) "This is a choice land, and whatsoever nation shall possess it shall be free from bondage, and from captivity, and from all other nations under heaven, if they will but serve the God of the land, who is Jesus Christ. . . ." (Ether 2:12.) The Book of Mormon chronicles the rise and fall of two mighty civilizations in America that failed to give heed to that decree and thus met with destruction.

2. Following the destruction of the civilizations that once inhabited this continent, God deliberately kept the American continent hidden until the Holy Roman Empire had broken up and the various nations had established themselves as independent kingdoms. Keeping America hidden until this time was no accident.

3. At the proper time, God inspired "a man among the Gentiles" who, by the Spirit of God, was led to rediscover the land of America and bring this rich new land to the attention of the people in Europe. That man, of course, was Christopher Columbus, who testified that he was inspired in what he did.

4. God revealed that shortly after the discovery of America, this nation would be colonized by peoples of Europe, called Gentiles, who would desire to escape the persecution and tyranny of the Old World. Book of Mormon prophets foretold the time when the Gentiles would scatter and kill the inhabitants of the land whom we know today as the Indian nations.

5. God revealed over 2500 years ago that the kingdoms of Europe would try to exercise dominion over the colonists who had fled to America, that this would lead to a struggle for independence, and that the Colonists would win.

6. The Book of Mormon foretold the time when the colonists would establish this as a land of liberty that would not be governed by kings. The Lord declared that He would protect the land, and whoever would attempt to establish kings from within or without would perish.

7. God predicted through His prophets that this great Gentile nation, raised upon the American continent in these last days, would become the richest and most powerful on the face of the earth, even "above all other nations." (See 1 Nephi 13:15, 30.) It is evident from the vantage point of two hundred years of history that this country today has fulfilled in some measure that prophecy. No other country has been more richly blessed in terms of freedoms, money, and goods as the people of this nation.

The national celebration of our country's two-hundredth birthday has afforded The Church of Jesus Christ of Latter-day Saints a wonderful opportunity to reaffirm to the people of this nation the origin, purpose, and destiny of the United States of America. You may be interested in some of our efforts to instill this message among our own as well as others not of our faith.

As a part of our nation's Bicentennial celebration, the Tabernacle Choir toured the east coast, performing in Philadelphia, Boston, New York, and Washington, D.C. On July 3, 1976, the choir performed at the Kennedy Center to an overflow audience, with the president of the United States in attendance. Never have I felt so proud of this beloved country—and stirred with emotion—as when the choir performed those songs eulogizing our heritage and freedom.

For members of our church, an attractive publication was prepared for all Latter-day Saint families in the United States. This manual contained four lessons, designed especially for parents to teach their children in family home evenings the purpose and destiny of this land. In a recent report given to the Church by its Bicentennial chairman, it was reported that "the demand for this manual far exceeded our supply. In homes across America beautiful lessons have been taught on the purpose and destiny of this land." (L. Tom Perry, *Ensign,* November 1976, p. 39.)

For persons not of our church we have published a handsome booklet entitled *God's Hand in the Founding of America.* Three messages were emphasized within the pages of this attractive brochure: (1) that America's earliest history began more than 2,000 years ago and is contained in an ancient and sacred book called the Book of Mormon; (2) that the discovery of America and the establishment of the United States were part of God's plan and were brought about by men who were inspired and guided by God; and (3) that America's future destiny is dependent on the righteousness and morality of her families.

As a church, we are earnest about this message. We are most concerned about trends within this nation which, if unchecked and continued in their course, will lead us to the oblivion of former great civilizations. I speak of the trend of modern idolatry in our midst where men seem to venerate their possessions more than they do their God, who made this abundance possible. I speak of the trend of insatiable coveting where each person and group—business, labor, minority groups, and individuals—wants more and more but gives less and less. I speak of the desecration of the Sabbath day, which has degenerated into a national holiday for recreation. I speak of the break-up of families, where divorce has become an acceptable pattern in our society. As a church, we are appalled at the number of children who are left to grow up without *both* mother and father.

Yes, I speak of the moral permissiveness that has taken root in our midst. Today sex is all but deified, and yet is promenaded before our youth in its most explicit, coarsest, and debasing forms. Truly, in the words of Isaiah, we live in a time when men "call evil good, and good evil." (Isaiah 5:20.)

Yes, the Book of Mormon declares America to be "a land choice above all other lands," but we must remember the contingency of our freedom and prosperity. It is that we worship the God of this land— even Jesus Christ—and keep His commandments, or we shall meet the same fate of civilizations that have gone before us!

This nation is God-ordained for a glorious purpose. It is ordained as an ensign of liberty to all other nations. That liberty will be maintained as we keep the commandments of God. Righteousness, as the Book of Mormon states, is the indispensable ingredient to liberty.

A third theme evident in the Book of Mormon is that God has preserved throughout history a promised people, children of promise, because of special covenants that they or their progenitors have willfully made with God.

The history of a covenant people is recorded in the Bible and begins with Abraham. Therein we are told of special promises that God made to Abraham, Isaac, and Jacob. These promises subsequently were given to Jacob's twelve sons. Most are well-acquainted with the promise made to one of those sons, Judah, that the Messiah should come through his lineage. We are less familiar with the promise given to another of Jacob's sons, Joseph. If you will carefully read chapter 49 of Genesis, you will find these great promises given to Joseph and his posterity:

1. That Joseph's posterity would be numerous.
2. That his descendants would be sorely persecuted.
3. That his descendants would "run over a wall," the meaning of which I will comment on next.

The Book of Mormon tells the account of a colony of Israelites descended from Joseph, who left Jerusalem before its great destruction during the Babylonian siege under King Nebuchadnezzar. It tells how these descendants of Joseph "came over a wall," a metaphoric expression denoting a barrier to them. That barrier was the great ocean between the continents of Asia and America. The Book of Mormon tells how they were guided by the hand of the Lord to the land of America and how Joseph's posterity became very numerous on the land until they filled it with a mighty nation.

The patriarch to this family of Joseph in America was named Lehi, who said of himself, "I am a descendant of Joseph who was carried captive into Egypt. . . . great were the covenants of the Lord which he made unto Joseph." (2 Nephi 3:4.) He attempted to instruct all his posterity in these covenants. His eldest sons rebelled, but his younger sons kept the covenants. The division that occurred in Lehi's own family was in miniature what happened to Lehi's descendants who became a nation. Those who followed the dissident faction of Lehi's family called themselves Lamanites after the eldest son, Laman. Those who followed the more righteous branch of his family were called Nephites after the younger son, Nephi. The Book of Mormon chronicles many of the fratricidal wars that took place between these two groups and that eventually led to the destruction of their civilization when both factions grew in wickedness.

The American Indians are descendants, a remnant, from this once advanced civilization. Theirs is a noble and exalted heritage, a heritage that goes back over 2500 years on this promised land. Through the Book of Mormon their great heritage comes to light. Scholars have even come to recognize that the pre-Columbian Indian culture was far more advanced than historians had previously acknowledged. An example of this recognition is the work of the late Felix S. Cohen, prominent lawyer, philosopher, and recognized expert on Indian culture. In his essay "Americanizing the White Man," published in the *American Scholar* (Spring 1952, pp. 177-91), Mr. Cohen summarizes the contributions of the Indian to our modern society.

In the field of agriculture, Mr. Cohen states that "four-sevenths of our national farm produce is of plants domesticated or created by Indian botanists of pre-Columbian times." Their gifts to us in agriculture are corn, tobacco, white and sweet potatoes, beans, peanuts, tomatoes, pumpkins, chocolate, American cotton, and rubber.

In the field of medicine, the Indians' gift constituted, until a few years ago, "most of America's contributions to medical science." These are quinine, cocaine, witch hazel, oil of wintergreen, petroleum jelly, arnica, and others. Physicians and botanists "have not yet discovered a medicinal herb not known to the Indians."

But it is in the area of political science that the Indian may have made his greatest contribution. Thomas Jefferson freely acknowledged his debt to his Indian mentors. The fear in Jefferson's day was the aggrandizement of government power. Which is more preferable, the freedom of the Indian society or the oppression of European governments? Jefferson preferred the freedom of the Indian society. Then the question, Which submits man to the greatest evil? And Jefferson answered: "One who has seen both conditions of existence" would say the European form has the greatest evil. "The sheep are happier of themselves, than under the care of the wolves. It will be said that great societies cannot exist without government. The savages, therefore, break them into small ones."

And so the pattern of states within a nation that we call a federation of states, "the habit of treating chiefs as servants of the people instead of as masters, the insistence that the community must respect the diversity of their dreams—all these," according to Mr. Cohen, "were part of the American way of life before Columbus landed."

Before the destruction of the civilization from which the American Indian descended, Jesus Christ came to them. He said to these Israelites, "Ye are they of whom I said: other sheep I have which are not of this fold; them also I must bring, and they shall hear my voice. . . ." (3 Nephi 15:21.) These other sheep did hear His voice. He taught them His gospel. He foretold the fate that would befall their descendants, the Indian, many, many generations later.

"I have caused my people who are of the house of Israel to be smitten, and to be afflicted, and to be slain, and to be cast out from among [the Gentiles], and to become hated by them, and to be a hiss and a byword among them." (3 Nephi 16:9.)

In this remarkable prophecy, Jesus foretold not only what would happen to the Indian, but the sequence in which it would take place, namely, they would be afflicted, they would be slain, and they would be cast out. Modern history today verifies the accuracy of this prophecy.

This prophecy states that the Indian would first be afflicted. What was the nature of that affliction? Before the white man came to this continent, North America was almost totally free from infectious disease. There was no smallpox, no measles, no mumps, no cholera, no diphtheria or tuberculosis. It was only after the white man came that the Indian contracted these diseases. Smallpox was the most deadly of these afflictions. More Indians succumbed to smallpox than fell casualty in all their wars with the United States. The Cheyennes lost half their tribe from smallpox. The Mandans were almost exterminated. The Crees, it is said, lost seven thousand. A quarter of the Pawnees were killed by the epidemic, and estimates of deaths among the Blackfoot run as high as eight thousand.

Later, thousands of Indians died of respiratory diseases brought by low resistance to white man's diseases. This was the period when pneumonia and tuberculosis took such a toll that the Indians were called the "vanishing Americans."

The prophecy by the Savior further states that the Indian would be slain. Between 1800 and 1860, it is estimated the Indian population decreased from one million to 44,000. The figures are rough estimates, but they do gauge the great losses sustained by the Indian nations owing to disease, wars, and government policies. Yes, thousands of Indians were slain, chiefly through massacres and the Indian wars. Remember some of these wars and famous Indian Chiefs: Black Hawk's War; the Little Crow uprising; the Apache and Navajo wars; Chief Crazy Horse and the Sioux battles; Sitting Bull and the Battle of Little Big Horn; Chief Joseph and the Nez Perce; the Wounded Knee massacres.

Last, the prophecy by Jesus declared that the Indian would be cast out from among the Gentiles. From 1778 to 1871 it is said that the United States government signed and ratified 371 treaties with the Indian nations, and each was broken or rescinded. The most infamous of these laws was the Indian Removal Act of 1830. American society swept to the Mississippi River and completely surrounded the five civilized tribes, who were allowed to live in peace for a time; but then agitation against them increased, and finally by the Act of 1830, these people were removed from their homes to the land west of the Mississippi. As the Indians were evicted from their homes—"cast out," to use the phrase of the Lord's prophecy—thousands of the old, the weak, and the young perished. The five "civilized" tribes that made this death march, called the "Trail of Tears," were the Cherokees, Choctaws, Creeks, Chickasaws, and Seminoles. It is said that one quarter of the tribe of Cherokees, 4,000 in number, died in the march.

These "civilized tribes," so-called because they lived in houses and built farms, were settled in Oklahoma, with the exception of the Seminoles. This was to be their territory, never to be preempted by the whites. Despite this promise, however, Oklahoma became the forty-sixth state of the Union, and the Indians were pushed out or placed on reservations. When oil was discovered in that state, ironically the richest deposits were discovered in the territory that had been given to the Indians. Because their land had been usurped, it was necessary to take their claim into federal court. The attorney who represented the case for the Indians was Ernest L. Wilkinson, a member of The Church of Jesus Christ of Latter-day Saints and past president of Brigham Young University. The settlement was one of the largest in legal history and made some of the Indian people in Oklahoma among the richest in the nation.

In spite of afflictions, deaths, and inequities done to the Indian people over the years, yet they remain children of promise. Listen to their promise contained in the Book of Mormon: ". . . it shall come to pass that they [the Indians] shall be driven and scattered by the Gentiles; and after they have been driven and scattered by the Gentiles, behold, then will the Lord remember the covenant which he made unto Abraham and unto all the house of Israel." (Mormon 5:29.) ". . . then shall the remnant [among whom are the American Indians] . . . know concerning us [the Book of Mormon civilization], how that we came out from Jerusalem. . . . the gospel of Jesus Christ shall be declared among them; wherefore, they shall be restored unto the knowledge of their fathers, and also to the knowledge of Jesus Christ, which was had among their fathers. And then shall they rejoice; for they shall know that it is a blessing unto them from the hand of God." (2 Nephi 30:4-6.)

"Wherefore, I will consecrate this land unto thy seed [meaning the modern remnant of Israel] . . . forever, for the land of their inheritance; for it is a choice land, . . . above all other lands. . . ." (2 Nephi 10:19.)

Such is the promise by God to this favored remnant of Joseph today.

But what of the Gentiles, descendants of the European colonists who migrated to this land? What is their promise? Of these favored people, those who populate our great land today, the Savior prophesied: ". . . if they will repent and hearken unto my words, and harden not their hearts, I will establish my church among them, and they shall come in unto the covenant and be numbered among this the remnant of Jacob, unto whom I have given this land for their inheritance. . . ." (3 Nephi 21:22.)

I humbly testify that God has mercifully fulfilled this promise to the Gentiles. His church, The Church of Jesus Christ of Latter-day Saints, has been established among them. Thankfully, thousands have come into the Church where they, too, will receive the blessings promised by God to Abraham's posterity.

Humbly I witness that I know the certainty of the truth of this message. I testify to the truthfulness of the Book of Mormon as being the word of God. Jesus Christ does live, and He will return again to this earth. A special destiny awaits those who are righteous and will abide by His covenants.

XVII

A Message to Judah from Joseph

"Our affinity toward modern Judah is not prompted out of mutual suffering; it is prompted out of a knowledge of our peculiar relationships together—relationships that claim a common heritage."

There is a great affinity for the Jews by the Mormons. The Jews have endured great persecution and suffering. This we understand, for our people have also undergone severe persecution and extermination. Indeed, the man we revere as a modern prophet, Joseph Smith, was martyred for his testimony in 1844. In 1846 our people had to leave the United States in exodus because of the threat of annihilation. We settled in a desert region similar to the topography around the Dead Sea and the Sea of Galilee. There we developed our "land of promise." Yes, we can empathize with the suffering of the Jews, for we have co-suffered with them. But our affinity toward modern Judah is not prompted out of mutual suffering; it is prompted out of a knowledge of our peculiar relationships together—relationships that claim a common heritage. Jeremiah has prophesied that in the latter times, "the house of Judah shall walk with the house of Israel, and they shall come together. . . ." (Jeremiah 3:18.)

We need to know more about the Jews, and the Jews ought to know more about the Mormons. When we understand one another, then perhaps we will understand why David Ben Gurion said to me on one of my visits to Tel Aviv, "There are no people in the world who understand the Jews like the Mormons."

Among the kindred doctrines of the Mormons and the Jews is our mutual belief in Jehovah, a God of revelation. We share a common belief in the Messiah who will come. We further hold reciprocal beliefs in prophets. We hold a common commitment to the return of the Jews to the "land of Jerusalem," in fulfillment of the words of the ancient prophets. There are many other doctrinal and social similarities.

The foundation of The Church of Jesus Christ of Latter-day Saints is a belief in revelation—modern revelation by God of His purposes and directions to living prophets. We believe as Amos declared: "Surely the Lord God will do nothing, but he revealeth his secret unto his servants the prophets." (Amos 3:7.) We declare that secrets, long since hidden through the ages, have been revealed again through a prophet by the revelation of "a new and everlasting covenant" to Israel. That prophet's name was Joseph Smith. These are the words of his own testimony:

"On the evening on the 21st of September, A.D. 1823, while I was praying unto God, and endeavoring to exercise faith in the precious promises of Scripture, on a sudden a light like that of day, only of a far purer and more glorious appearance and brightness, burst into the room, indeed the first sight was as though the house was filled with consuming fire; the appearance produced a shock that affected the whole body; in a moment a personage stood before me surrounded with a glory yet greater than that with which I was already surrounded. This messenger proclaimed himself to be an angel of God, sent to bring the joyful tidings that the covenant which God made with ancient Israel was at hand to be fulfilled. . . . I was informed that I was chosen to be an instrument in the hands of God to bring about some of His purposes in this glorious dispensation." (*History of the Church* 4:536-37.)

From the very inception of this latter-day work, which claims to be a restoration of the covenants given by God to Abraham, Isaac, and Jacob, the Church has had a deep interest in the remnant of the house of Israel, the descendants of Judah.

In 1836, the Saints completed their first temple at Kirtland, Ohio. In the dedicatory prayer offered on that occasion, Joseph Smith petitioned the "Lord God of Israel":

"O Lord . . . thou knowest that thou hast a great love for the children of Jacob, who have been scattered upon the mountains for a long time. . . .

"We therefore ask thee to have mercy upon the children of Jacob, that Jerusalem, from this hour, may begin to be redeemed;

"And the yoke of bondage may begin to be broken off from the house of David;

"And the children of Judah may begin to return to the lands which thou didst give to Abraham, their father." (D&C 109:60-64.)

This was said during the Passover Season, March 27, 1836.

Before the Prophet was killed, he dispatched a Jewish apostle by the name of Orson Hyde to dedicate the land of Palestine for the return of the Jews. This concern for a homeless people and the sending of this apostle were done at a time when the Mormons themselves were virtually homeless, having been dispossessed of their lands and possessions in Missouri. Orson Hyde left on his assignment in the fall of 1840 and arrived in Palestine in October 1841. On October 24, 1841, he ascended the Mount of Olives alone, built an altar to the Lord, and offered a dedicatory prayer. Here are some portions of that prayer:

> Thy servant . . . has safely arrived in this place *to dedicate and consecrate this land unto Thee, for the gathering together of Judah's scattered remnants, according to the predictions of the holy Prophets—for the building up of Jerusalem* again after it has been trodden down by the Gentiles so long, *and for rearing a Temple* in honor of Thy name. . . .
>
> O Thou, Who didst covenant with Abraham, Thy friend, and Who didst renew that covenant with Isaac, and confirm the same with Jacob with an oath, that Thou wouldst not only give them this land for an everlasting inheritance, but that Thou wouldst also remember their seed forever. Abraham, Isaac, and Jacob have long since closed their eyes in death, and made the grave their mansion. Their children are scattered and dispersed abroad among the nations of the Gentiles like sheep that have no shepherd, and are still looking forward for the fulfillment of those promises which Thou didst make concerning them. . . .
>
> . . . Let the land become abundantly fruitful when possessed by its rightful heirs; let it again flow with plenty to feed the returning prodigals. . . . *Incline them to gather in upon this land according to Thy word. Let them come like clouds and like doves to their windows.* [This was uttered before the airplane was invented.] *Let the large ships of the nations bring them* from the distant isles; and let kings become their nursing fathers, and queens with motherly fondness wipe the tear of sorrow from their eye.
>
> . . . Let them know that it is Thy good pleasure to restore the kingdom unto Israel—raise up Jerusalem as its capital, and *constitute her people a distinct nation and government,* with David Thy servant, even a descendant from the loins of ancient David to be their king. (*History of the Church* 4:456-57. Italics added.)

This was said at a time when Jewish immigration was but a trickle. Today the gathering has been realized in part with over three million Jews back in the land of their fathers.

Historically, we must recognize that interest in the restoration of the Jews to their homeland is older than modern Zionism and the great work of Theodor Herzl and others. There were a number of Christian sects in the nineteenth century that held millennial views and saw the return of the Jews to their homeland as a "sign of the times" that would precede the second advent of Jesus Christ. The Mormon interest was and is more than this. Our concern and interest are a kinship to our Jewish brothers.

Our common heritage goes back to Abraham, Isaac, and Jacob. God reiterated to Jacob the same promises given to Abraham, and then gave Jacob the new name of Israel. His posterity—all those who descended through his twelve sons—were known by this designation.

They were variously referred to as the "house of Israel," "Children of Israel," or "Tribes of Israel." Though all of his posterity received the family name designation through the twelve sons, today it has become common practice to identify only one of his twelve sons, Judah, with the family designation, Israelite, because they have maintained their separate identity.

Jacob, or Israel, pronounced blessings on each of his twelve sons. Each was given a peculiar and distinctive blessing. Of special significance were the blessings pronounced on Judah and Joseph. To Joseph, Jacob said:

"Joseph is a fruitful bough, even a fruitful bough by a well; whose branches run over the wall:

"The archers have sorely grieved him, and shot at him, and hated him:

"But his bow abode in strength, and the arms of his hands were made strong by the hands of the mighty God of Jacob; (from thence is the shepherd, the stone of Israel:)

"Even by the God of thy father, who shall help thee; and by the Almighty, who shall bless thee with blessings of heaven above, blessings of the deep that lieth under, blessings of the breasts, and of the womb:

"The blessings of thy father have prevailed above the blessings of my progenitors unto the utmost bound of the everlasting hills: they shall be on the head of Joseph, and on the crown of the head of him that was separate from his brethren." (Genesis 49:22-26.)

There are several points which we should note carefully about this blessing:

1. Joseph's posterity would be numerous, that is, he would be a "fruitful bough."

2. His posterity or "branches" would "run over a wall."

3. His descendants would be sorely persecuted, the meaning of the phraseology, "the archers have sorely grieved him, and shot at him, and hated him."

4. The blessings on Joseph's posterity were to prevail "above the blessings of my progenitors unto the utmost bound of the everlasting hills."

Later I shall comment on the interpretation of this blessing as it affects the relationships of the present-day Mormons and Jews, but first it will be instructive to review the history of the descendants of Israel after they came into the land promised to Abraham as "the land of Canaan . . . an everlasting possession." (Genesis 17:8.)

For a time the confederated tribes were a united monarchy under

Saul, David, and Solomon, but ultimately they divided into two major kingdoms. The kingdom to the north, which comprised ten and one-half tribes including the descendants of Joseph, retained the designation Israel. The kingdom to the south, made up primarily of the tribe of Judah, adopted the name of Judah. (See 1 Kings 11:31-32; 12:19-24.)

Prophets were raised up among these two nations to call them to repentance because of their idolatry and wickedness. The prophet Amos predicted the results of this disobedience to God. "Now shall they [Israel] go captive with the first that go captive. . . ." (Amos 6:7.) "I will sift the house of Israel among all nations, like as corn is sifted in a sieve, yet shall not the least grain fall upon the earth." (Amos 9:9.)

The northern kingdom, Israel, was subsequently taken into captivity by the Assyrians 721 years B.C. The Old Testament contains no history of Israel nor of Joseph's descendants after this date. Are we to believe that God's promises to Joseph were for naught, that the prophecy of his posterity being numerous, "running over a wall," being sorely persecuted, and going to the "utmost bound of the everlasting hills" would not be fulfilled?

Because of the division that occurred between the two kingdoms, the Lord made special provision that separate records be kept. The prophet Ezekiel spoke of these records:

"The word of the Lord came again unto me, saying,

"Moreover, thou son of man, take thee one stick, and write upon it, For Judah, and for the children of Israel his companions: then take another stick, and write upon it, For Joseph, the stick of Ephraim, and for all the house of Israel his companions:

"And join them one to another into one stick; and they shall become one in thine hand,

"And when the children of thy people shall speak unto thee, saying, Wilt thou not shew us what thou meanest by these?

"Say unto them, Thus saith the Lord God; Behold, I will take the stick of Joseph, which is in the hand of Ephraim, and the tribes of Israel his fellows, and will put them with him, even with the stick of Judah, and make them one stick, and they shall be one in mine hand.

"And the sticks whereon thou writest shall be in thine hand before their eyes." (Ezekiel 37:15-20.)

From this commandment from God to Ezekiel, these provisions should be noted: (1) that a stick or record be kept for Judah and a stick or record be kept for Joseph; and (2) that the two records be joined together into one record in the hands of that prophet.

Where is the fulfillment of this important commandment? Who claims to have the record of Joseph today?

The record of Joseph has been brought forth in this day to Joseph Smith by a messenger sent from God. That record is called the Book of Mormon, named after one of the seed of Joseph who abridged the records of his people.

The records of these people lay buried in the earth for centuries, until a heavenly messenger turned them over to Joseph Smith in 1827. They were subsequently translated from their ancient reformed Egyptian writing into the English language and were published to the world in the year 1830.

But what about the prophecies that pertain to the house of Judah? The northern tribes of Israel were not the only ones to be dispersed according to prophecy. Judah, the southern kingdom, was also to be scattered: "And the Lord said, I will remove Judah also out of my sight, as I have removed Israel, and will cast off this city Jerusalem which I have chosen, and the house of which I said, My name shall be there." (2 Kings 23:37.)

The history of the scattering of the nation Judah is so well known as to be regarded proverbial. Under the seizure of Babylon, the nation was taken into exile. A remnant returned to rebuild Jerusalem and the temple after the Persians came into power. Since that time, except for a short period of independence under the Maccabbees, Judah has been under the yoke of foreign domination: the Macedonian Empire; the tripartite government rule by Egypt, Syria, and Macedonia; Syrian domination; the Roman rule; and a final dispersion among all nations.

Space will not permit extensive comment about the depth of the suffering and persecution of the Jews among many nations. Some of the most evil of those deeds were perpetrated upon the remaining Jews in Palestine in the name of Christianity during the Crusades. Will Durant has written of this sad chapter of human suffering, "No other people has ever known so long an exile, or so hard a fate."

I remember standing on the ruins of what was the largest Jewish ghetto in Europe in the Jewish section of Warsaw, Poland, in August 1946. There we were given a description of what had transpired as being somewhat typical of that which had gone on in various parts of Europe through the establishment of the medieval ghetto.

There 250,000 descendants of Judah had lived prior to the war. Under the Nazi rule, through forced labor, Jews were required to build a wall around the ghetto. Later some 150,000 Jews from other parts of Europe were brought into that area. The Germans first tried to starve them out, but when that did not work, they transported over 310,000 of them to extermination camps. When Heinrich Himmler found that there were still some 60,000 Jews alive in the ghetto, he ordered their "resettlement." When they forcibly resisted, the German S.S. General Stroop ordered tanks, artillery, flame throwers, and dynamite squads on the ghetto. The extermination that was to have taken three days lasted four weeks. The final report by the general read, "Total number of Jews dealt with: 56,065, including both Jews caught and Jews whose extermination can be proved." This report left 36,000 Jews unaccounted for, who were no doubt claimed by the gas chambers. (William L. Shirer, *The Rise and Fall of the Third Reich,* Greenwich, Conn.: Fawcett Publications, 1959, p. 1272.)

As we stood on the crumbled brick and mortar and the rubble some fifteen feet deep, with only the spire of one burned synagogue showing, we were told that thousands of bodies still remained under the rubble of those once great buildings in this section of Warsaw.

I have visited some of the concentration camps, the mass graves, and the crematoriums, where, it is estimated, six million of the sons and daughters of Judah lost their lives, reducing their world population from seventeen to eleven million. I have been impressed to tears as I have visited some of these wanderers, those persecuted and driven sons of our Heavenly Father, my brethren of Judah.

Yes, the prophecies regarding the dispersion and suffering of Judah have been fulfilled. But the gathering and reestablishment of the Jews was also clearly predicted. This predicted gathering has three phases: the gathering of Israel to the land of Zion, the Western Hemisphere; the return of the ten tribes from the north countries; and the reestablishment of the Jews in Palestine, which had been long ago predicted by the prophets in these words:

"It shall come to pass in that day, that the Lord shall set his hand again the second time to recover the remnant of his people, . . . And he shall set up an ensign for the nations, and shall assemble the outcasts of Israel, and gather together the dispersed of Judah from the four corners of the earth." (Isaiah 11:11-12.)

"For, lo, the days come, saith the Lord, that I will bring again the captivity of my people Israel and Judah, . . . and I will cause them to return to the land that I gave to their fathers, and they shall possess it." (Jeremiah 30:3.)

"Behold, the days come, saith the Lord, that I will make a new covenant with the house of Israel, and with the house of Judah." (Jeremiah 31:31.)

"I will strengthen the house of Judah, and I will save the house of Joseph, and I will bring them again to place them; . . . I will hiss for them, and gather them; for I have redeemed them. . . ." (Zechariah 10:6, 8.)

The Book of Mormon is no less explicit in its prophecy concerning Israel's and Judah's gathering from a long dispersion:

"And it shall come to pass that they shall be gathered in from their long dispersion, from the isles of the sea, and from the four parts of the earth; and the nations of the Gentiles shall be great in the eyes of me, saith God, in carrying them forth to the lands of their inheritance.

"Yea, the kings of the Gentiles shall be nursing fathers unto them, and their queens shall become nursing mothers. . . ." (2 Nephi 10:8-9.)

I saw the fulfillment of this prophecy with my own eyes in wartorn Europe in 1946 when ships of Great Britain smuggled the Jews to Palestine in response to the powerful spirit of gathering. The Mormon people understand this spirit.

Here is a further prophecy from the Book of Mormon regarding the scattering and the restoration of Judah:

"Wherefore, the Jews shall be scattered among all nations; yea, and also Babylon shall be destroyed; wherefore, the Jews shall be scattered by other nations.

"And after they have been scattered, and the Lord God hath scourged them by other nations for the space of many generations, . . . the Lord will set his hand again the second time to restore his people from their lost and fallen state. Wherefore, he will proceed to do a marvelous work and a wonder among the children of men." (2 Nephi 25:15-17.)

Since 1948, the people of the world have witnessed a marvelous drama taking place before their eyes, and yet it is a miracle that has gone rather unnoticed and unappreciated. One of the greatest events in history is the literal gathering of the Jews to their homeland from "the four corners of the earth." It is, as Isaiah prophesied, "a marvelous work and a wonder."

In 1950, I said, "There has been much confusion over the Palestine question—much talk of division of the land, of quotas, import restrictions—but out of it all I cannot help feeling that we will see a complete fulfilment of the prophecies which have been made regarding this people. These prophecies are in rapid course of fulfilment before our very eyes today." (*Conference Report,* April 1950, p. 77.) Since that time, the nation of Israel has fought three wars, regained Jerusalem and the Western Wall (Wailing Wall), and added the Golan Heights and much of the Sinai Peninsula to its territory.

We previously considered the blessing that Jacob, or Israel, pronounced on Joseph. Let us now consider the blessing pronounced on Judah:

"Judah, thou art he whom thy brethren shall praise: thy hand shall be in the neck of thine enemies; thy father's children shall bow down before thee.

"Judah is a lion's whelp: from the prey, my son, thou art gone up: he stooped down, he couched as a lion, and as an old lion; who shall rouse him up?

"The sceptre shall not depart from Judah, nor a lawgiver from between his feet, until Shiloh come; and unto him shall the gathering of the people be.

"Binding his foal unto the vine, and his ass's colt unto the choice vine; he washed his garments in wine, and his clothes in the blood of grapes:

"His eyes shall be red with wine, and his teeth white with milk." (Genesis 49:8-12.)

The great blessing to Judah is that it contemplated the coming of Shiloh who would gather His people to Him. This prophecy concerning Shiloh has been subject to several rabbinic and Christian interpretations and the object of considerable controversy. The interpretation given this passage by the Latter-day Saints is one based on revelation to modern prophets, not on scholarly commentary. It was revealed to Joseph Smith that Shiloh is the Messiah. (See Genesis 50:24, Inspired Version.)

President Wilford Woodruff, the apostle who became the fourth President of the Church, said this to the Jews in the year 1879:

> And this is the will of your great Elohim, O house of Judah, and whenever you shall be called upon to perform this work, the God of Israel will help you. You have a great future and destiny before you and you cannot avoid fulfilling it; you are the royal chosen seed, and the God of your father's house has kept you distinct as a nation for eighteen hundred years, under all the oppression of the whole Gentile world. You may not wait until you believe on Jesus of Nazareth, but when you meet with *Shiloh* your king, you will know him; your destiny is marked out, you cannot avoid it. It is true that after you return and gather your nation home, and rebuild your City and Temple, that the Gentiles may gather together their armies to go against you to battle. . . . When this affliction comes, the living God, that led Moses through the wilderness, will deliver you, and *your Shiloh will come* and stand in your midst and will fight your battles; and you will know him, and the afflictions of the Jews will be at an end, while the destruction of the Gentiles will be so great that it will take the whole house of Israel who are gathered about Jerusalem, seven months to bury the dead of their enemies, and the weapons of war will last them seven years for fuel, so that they need not go to any forest for wood. These are tremendous sayings—who can bear them? Nevertheless they are true, and will

be fulfilled, according to the sayings of Ezekiel, Zechariah and other prophets. Though the heavens and the earth pass away, not one jot or tittle will fall unfulfilled. (Matthias F. Cowley, *The Life of Wilford Woodruff*, pp. 509-10.)

The Book of Mormon, which was also written to the Jew, testifies who Shiloh is, "for there is save one Messiah spoken of by the prophets." (2 Nephi 25:18.)

"The sceptre shall not depart from Judah, nor a lawgiver from between his feet, until Shiloh come." (Genesis 49:10.) We see the fulfillment of the Shiloh prophecy this way: Judah came to power when David was exalted to the throne. Even after the division of the northern and southern kingdoms, the kings of Judah sat on the throne. Following the Babylonian captivity, "lawgivers" were provided to the Jewish remnant who returned to Jerusalem. Zerubbabel, Ezra, and Nehemiah are examples. Subsequently the Sanhedrin was established, and it continued as the ruling body of the Jews until the destruction of Jerusalem and the scattering of the Jews. From that time, the Jews had no lawgiver to whom they could turn. Shiloh had come. He was Jesus of Nazareth, who was later crucified as "King of the Jews."

Christian history has emphasized the point that the Jews as a nation rejected their Messiah. Overlooked has been the fact that many Jews did believe him to be the Messiah. Among those Jews who did so were His twelve apostles and thousands of others who were converted by their ministry. We declare that after His ministry in Palestine, the resurrected Messiah personally visited the house of Joseph in this land of America, taught them, blessed them, and renewed the everlasting covenant with them. His ministry to America is recorded in the Book of Mormon.

You will recall the episode of Joseph and his brethren in the Old Testament, and how he was sold into Egypt. You will remember that, because of a famine in the land of Canaan, his brethren were compelled to go to Egypt to purchase corn from the granaries. Joseph had risen to the position of governor over the land and was in charge of those granaries. One of the most touching scenes recorded in the Torah is when Joseph made himself known to his brethren. "I am Joseph your brother. . . ." (Genesis 45:4.)

To our friends of modern Judah, we declare, "We are Joseph, your brothers." We claim kinship with them as descendants from our fathers, Abraham, Isaac, and Jacob. We belong to the same family. We, too, are the house of Israel.

There is yet another parallel to this story of Joseph. The brethren of Joseph in times past came to him during a famine for physical sustenance. Today there is another famine in the land, "not a famine of bread, nor a thirst for water, but of hearing the words of the Lord." (Amos 8:11.) Has not the Lord God said through Isaiah: "Everyone that thirsteth, come ye to the waters"? (Isaiah 55:1.) "[I will] satisfy thy soul in drought, and make fat thy bones: and thou shalt be like a watered garden, and like a spring of water, whose waters fail not." (Isaiah 58:11.)

We are also cognizant of God's charge to Judah through his prophet Jeremiah: "For my people have committed two evils: they have forsaken me the fountain of living waters, and hewed them out cisterns, broken cisterns, that can hold no water." (Jeremiah 2:13.)

Of far greater value than the physical sustenance that Joseph of old provided his brethren is the sustenance that modern Joseph has to offer modern Judah today. We offer freely bread to eat and water to drink. We come with a message and say, "We have 'living water' from its true source and well, which, if a man will drink it, 'shall be in him a well of living water, springing up into everlasting life.' " (See D&C 63:23.)

In Jacob's blessing to Judah, he declared: "Judah is . . . as an old lion; who shall rouse him up?" (Genesis 49:9.) We come as messengers bearing the legitimate authority to arouse Judah to her promises. We do not ask Judah to forsake her heritage. We are not asking her to leave father, mother, or family. We bring a message that Judah does not possess. That message constitutes "living water" from the Fountain of living water.

The Prophet Joseph Smith was given a commandment by the Lord to turn "the hearts of the Jews unto the prophet, and the prophets unto the Jews." (D&C 98:17.) We are presently sending our messengers to every land and people whose ideology permits us entrance. We have been gathering Joseph's descendants for nearly a century and a half. We hope those who are of Judah will not think it an intrusion for us to present our message to them. They are welcome to come to our meetings. We display no crosses. We collect no offerings. We honor each person's commitment to his unique heritage and individuality. We approach our friends and brothers in a different way than any other Christian church because we represent the restored covenant to the entire house of Israel.

Yes, we understand the Jews. We understand them because we belong to the same house of Israel. We are their brothers—Joseph. We look forward to the day of fulfilment of God's promise when "the house of Judah shall walk with the house of Israel." (Jeremiah 3:18.)

As one who, by special assignment, has been given authority in the house of Israel today, I ask the God of Abraham, Isaac, and Jacob to bless my brethren of Judah and have mercy on them; that the land to which Judah has returned after a long night of dispersion shall be fruitful, prosperous, and become the envy of her neighbors; that the nation Israel shall be delivered from all her oppressors and enemies; that Judah will "draw water out of the wells of salvation" and fulfill all those prophecies that God declared through His prophets Isaiah, Ezekiel, Jeremiah; and that "the Lord shall inherit Judah his portion in the holy land, and shall choose Jerusalem again." (Zechariah 2:12.)

XVIII

This Nation Shall Endure

"Let us rededicate ourselves to the lofty principles and practices of those wise men whom God raised up to give us our priceless freedom. Our liberties, our salvation, our well-being as a church and as a nation depend upon it."

I love this great nation of which we are a part. To me it is not just another nation, not just a member of the family of nations. It is a great and glorious nation with a divine mission, brought into being under the inspiration of heaven. It is truly a land choice above all others. I thank God for the knowledge we have regarding the prophetic history and the spiritual foundation of this great land of America.

When I contemplate the great events that have transpired here, going way back to the days when our first parents were placed in the Garden of Eden, and recall that this garden was here in America;

When I contemplate that it was here also that Adam met with a body of great high priests at Adam-ondi-Ahman shortly before his death and gave them his final blessing, and that to that same spot he is to return again to meet with the leaders of his people, his children;

When I contemplate that here in this land will be established the New Jerusalem, that here in this land Zion will be built;

When I contemplate that prophets of God anciently served here in this land, and that the resurrected Christ appeared to them;

When I contemplate that the greatest of all visions, the coming of God the Father and His Son, Jesus Christ, to the boy prophet, took place in this land;

When I contemplate all these marvelous things, my heart fills with gratitude that I am privileged to live here, and that I have the honor and pleasure not only of serving in the Church, but also of having served in the government of this great land. I consider it an honor and a privilege.

I am grateful for the Founding Fathers of this land and for the freedom they have vouchsafed to us. I am grateful that they recognized, as great leaders of this nation have always recognized, that the freedom we enjoy did not originate with the Founding Fathers; that these glorious principles, this great boon of freedom and respect for the dignity of man, came as a gift from the Creator. The Founding Fathers, it is true, welded together with superb genius the safeguards of these freedoms. It was necessary, however, for them to turn to the scriptures, to religion, in order to have their great experiment make sense to them. And so our freedom is God-given. It antedates the Founding Fathers. It is an eternal principle. It was a principle at issue in the spirit world.

I am grateful that the God of heaven saw fit to put His stamp of approval upon the Constitution and to indicate that it had come into being through wise men whom He raised up unto this very purpose. He asked the Saints, even in the dark days of their persecution and hardship, to continue to seek for redress from their enemies, "according," He said, "to the laws and constitution, . . . which I have suffered [or caused] to be established, and should be maintained for the rights and protection of all flesh. . . ." (D&C 101:77.) And then He made this most impressive declaration: "And for this purpose have I established the Constitution of this land, by the hands of wise men whom I raised up unto this very purpose, and redeemed the land by the shedding of blood." (D&C 101:80.)

It is gratifying that the constitutions in many of the other lands of our neighbors in the Americas are patterned very much after this divinely appointed constitution, which the God of heaven directed in the founding of this great nation. It is not any wonder, therefore, that Joseph Smith the Prophet, a truly great American patriot, said, referring to the Constitution, "[It] is a glorious standard; it is founded in the wisdom of God. It is a heavenly banner. . . ." (*Teachings of the Prophet Joseph Smith,* p. 147.)

President Brigham Young declared prophetically, "When the day comes in which the Kingdom of God will bear rule, the flag of the United States will proudly flutter unsullied on the flagstaff of liberty and equal rights, without a spot to sully its fair surface; the glorious flag our fathers have bequeathed to us will then be unfurled to the breeze by those who have power to hoist it aloft and defend its sanctity." (*Journal of Discourses* 2:317.) But, President Young asks, "How long will it be before the words of the Prophet Joseph will be fulfilled? He said if the Constitution of the United States were saved at all it must be done by these people. It will not be many years before these words come to pass." (*JD* 12:204.) These words were spoken April 8, 1868, over one hundred years ago.

Yes, we have a rich heritage, but may I remind you that nations ofttimes sow the seeds of their own destruction even while enjoying unprecedented prosperity, even before reaching the zenith or the peak of their power. I think history clearly indicates that this is often the case. When it appears that all is well, ofttimes the very seeds of destruction are sown, sometimes unwittingly. Most of the great civilizations of the world have not been conquered from without until they have destroyed themselves from within by sowing these seeds.

It is my conviction that God does now look with favor, and has looked with favor, upon this government, which He established by wise men. It is also my firm conviction that His protective hand is still over the United States of America. I know, too, that if we will keep the commandments of God—live as He has directed and does now direct, through His prophets—we will continue to have His protecting hand over us. But we must be true to the eternal verities, the great Christian virtues that God has revealed. Then, and only then, will we be safe as a nation and as individuals. God grant that the faithfulness of the Latter-day Saints will provide the balance of power to save this nation in time of crisis.

In 1973 the First Presidency said: "We urge members of the Church and all Americans to begin now to reflect more intently on the meaning and importance of the Constitution, and of adherence to its principles. . . . In these challenging days, when there are so many influences which would divert us, there is a need to rededicate ourselves to the lofty principles and practices of our founding fathers. . . ." (*Church News,* September 22, 1973, p. 3.)

Let us not permit these admonitions of our living prophets to fall on deaf ears. Let us, as they direct, learn the meaning and importance of our God-ordained Constitution. Let us rededicate ourselves to the lofty principles and practices of those wise men whom God raised up to give us our priceless freedom. Our liberties, our salvation, our well-being as a church and as a nation depend upon it.

This nation does have a spiritual foundation—a prophetic history. Every true Latter-day Saint should love the United States of America, the most generous nation under heaven, the Lord's base of operations in these last days.

May we do all in our power to strengthen and safeguard this base and increase our freedom. This nation will endure. It may cost blood, but it is God-ordained for a glorious purpose. We must never forget that the gospel message we bear to the world is to go forth to the world from this nation, and that gospel message can prosper only in an atmosphere of freedom. We must maintain and strengthen our freedom in this blessed land.

May God bless America and preserve our divine Constitution and the Republic that He established thereunder.

Index